INTRODUCING

JAZZ for the ROCK GUITARIST

Stretch the Boundaries of Your Playing

ROBERT BROWN

Acquisition, editorial, music typesetting, interior design: Nathaniel Gunod, Workshop Arts
Cover photograph: Jeff Oshiro Cover design: Ted Engelbart and Martha Widmann

TABLE OF CONTENTS

ABOUT THE AUTHOR

Robert Brown, guitarist and composer, was on the faculty of the National Guitar Summer Workshop from 1984 to 1991. During those years, he taught everything from blues to jazz, songwriting and MIDI seminars. He is the author of many other books published by the National Guitar Workshop and Alfred. Robert Brown is currently living and working in Washington, D.C.

INTRODUCTION

This book is designed to bring you, the rock guitarist, into the world of jazz guitar. It will help you make the chords you play sound jazzier, the solos you play sound hipper, and it will also help you to understand some of the theoretical concepts that are frequently used by jazz players.

The first section of the book is a Theory Review which covers topics such as the chromatic scale, intervals, major scales, minor scales, triads, and complex chords. Don't pass this section by, even if you think you know all about these topics. I am sure there will be some new things for you to learn!

The rest of the book is devoted to Harmony and Soloing. You'll learn diatonic 7th chords, many other "jazz" chords, blues progressions, new pentatonic-type lines, and some very hip minor lines, not to mention the theory behind all of these concepts.

A WORD ABOUT STYLE

Here are some things to keep in mind that will help you capture the jazz style:

1) Start off with a clean sound.
2) Think melodically. Try to make up melodies when you solo.
3) Think about repeating patterns when you solo.
4) Vary your rhythms. Alternate between:
    a) Straight eighth notes - all the eighths have equal value.
    b) Eighth-note triplets - three equal eighths played in one beat.
    c) Swing or Jazz eighths - the first eighth of each pair is twice as long as the second eighth.

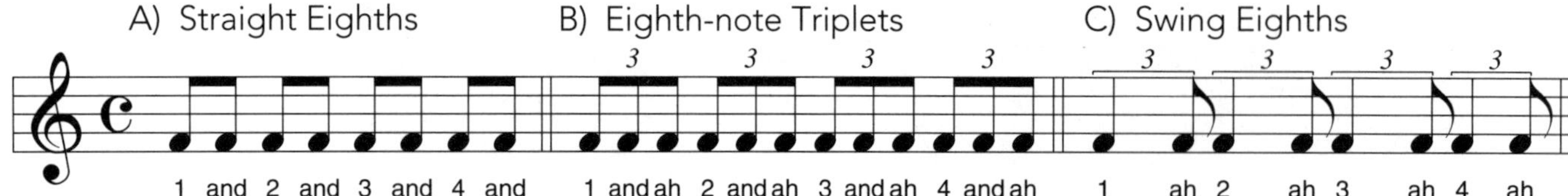

I hope that you will enjoy studying the ideas in this book. My advice is to GO SLOWLY! Make sure that you fully understand, and are able to play everything on a page before you go on to the next page. After you have gone through the book completely and thoroughly, you can always come back to any topic or lesson and study it again. Each page is a lesson, and often several pages will be devoted to the same topic.

HAVE FUN!

THEORY REVIEW

THE CHROMATIC SCALE

The Chromatic Scale is made with twelve ascending or descending half-steps. A half-step is the smallest distance between two notes. On the guitar, this is the distance between two adjacent frets. You can play the chromatic scale a number of different ways. One good way to practice is to start on any open string and play each fret up to the twelfth. The important thing to remember is that the note that you start on becomes the first scale degree (1) which is also called the root. All the other notes are given scale degree numbers based on their distance from the root.

EXAMPLE 1

A common fingering for the chromatic scale

EXAMPLE 2

ENHARMONIC EQUIVALENTS

Each note in the chromatic scale has both a letter name and a scale degree number. In fact, when you are ascending from C, some of the notes have sharps ♯ in front of them, but when you are descending from C, those same notes have flats ♭. That means that some notes can have two names! These are said to be *enharmonic equivalents*. In the C Chromatic scale, there are five pairs of enharmonic notes:

C♯ and D♭	or	♯1 and ♭2
D♯ and E♭	or	♯2 and ♭3
F♯ and G♭	or	♯4 and ♭5
G♯ and A♭	or	♯5 and ♭6
A♯ and B♭	or	♯6 and ♭7

The enharmonic spellings you will use depend upon the key you are in, whether the music is ascending or descending, and the *intervals* involved. The following sections on intervals and scales will clarify this concept.

INTERVALS

The distance between any two notes is called an interval. The smallest interval is the half-step, which is the distance between any two adjacent frets on the guitar. The next largest interval is called the *whole-step*, which is equal to two half-steps, or a move of two frets on the guitar. In one octave, the following intervals will occur (they can all be measured in half-steps):

Scale Degrees	Interval	Half-Steps	
1 to ♭2	minor 2nd	1	
1 to 2	major 2nd	2	
1 to ♭3	minor 3rd	3	
1 to 3	major 3rd	4	
1 to 4	perfect 4th	5	
1 to ♯4	augmented 4th	6	} *Enharmonic*
1 to ♭5	diminished 5th	6	
1 to 5	perfect 5th	7	
1 to ♯5	augmented 5th	8	} *Enharmonic*
1 to ♭6	minor 6th	8	
1 to 6	major 6th	9	} *Enharmonic*
1 to 𝄫7*	diminished 7th	9	
1 to ♭7	minor 7th	10	
1 to 7	major 7th	11	
1 to 8	perfect octave	12	

*𝄫 = *Double flat.* A double flat lowers the note one whole-step.

THE MAJOR SCALE

A scale is a group of notes which follow each other in some sort of step-wise order, usually using half-steps and whole-steps. There are many scales in existence and perhaps the most important of them for rock and jazz musicians is the major scale. It has a specific arrangement of half- and whole-steps that is always the same, no matter which note you start on. The order is always the same.

So, the formula for a major scale in whole- and half-steps is:

= Whole-step

Whole Whole Half Whole Whole Whole Half

= Half-step

The half-steps are between 3 and 4, and 7 and 8.

The C Major scale

EXAMPLE 3

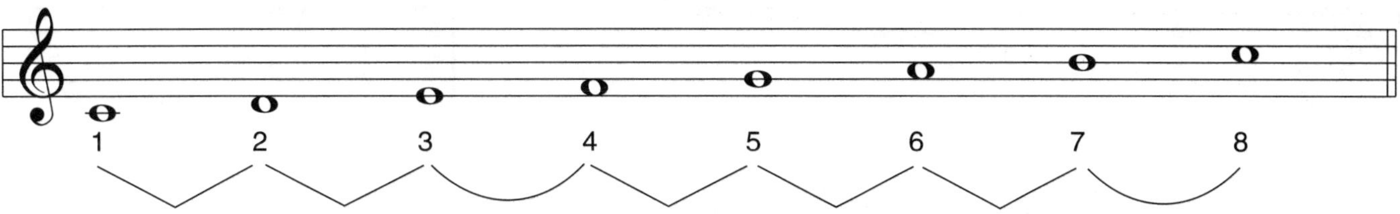

The E♭ Major scale

EXAMPLE 4

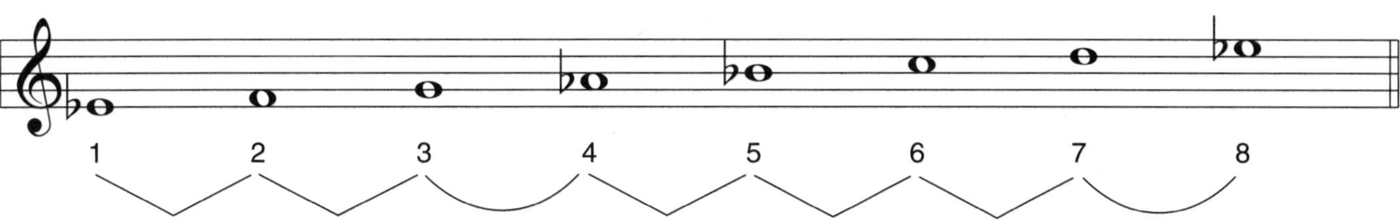

As you can see from the two scales above, the intervals between scale degrees is constant from key to key. No matter what note you start on, the intervals will always be the same. The notes that result from building a major scale on a particular root note comprise the key of that root. For instance, the notes in the E♭ Major scale are the notes that make up the key of E♭ Major.

ROMAN NUMERALS

Roman numerals are commonly used to indicate frets and to represent harmonies. Since you'll be seeing a lot of them in this book, here is a quick review of Roman numerals and their Arabic equivalents:

I	II	III	IV	V	VI	VII	VII	IX	X	XI	XII	XIII	XIV	XV
1	2	3	4	5	6	7	8	9	10	11	12	13	14	15

MAJOR SCALE FINGERINGS

There are six different fingerings for the major scale on the guitar. With these six fingerings, you can play in any key six different ways. Just learn all six fingerings. You can start any one of them on any note, so you can instantly play in any major key on any part of the neck! Each fingering can be named according to the finger and string that begin the scale [finger/string]. Each of the six fingerings will be shown in second position. It is called second position because your first finger plays at the second fret. Second position is comprised of the second, third, fourth and fifth frets.

C Major 2/5

EXAMPLE 5

In this fingering, the 2/5 means that you start with your second finger on the fifth string. Since this one is in the key of C, we will start on the third fret, because that is where we find a C on the fifth string. Keep your hand in second position (with your first finger on the second fret) and when you get to the first fret F on the first string, just stretch out your first finger to grab that note. This is marked with "str." underneath the TAB in the fingerings.

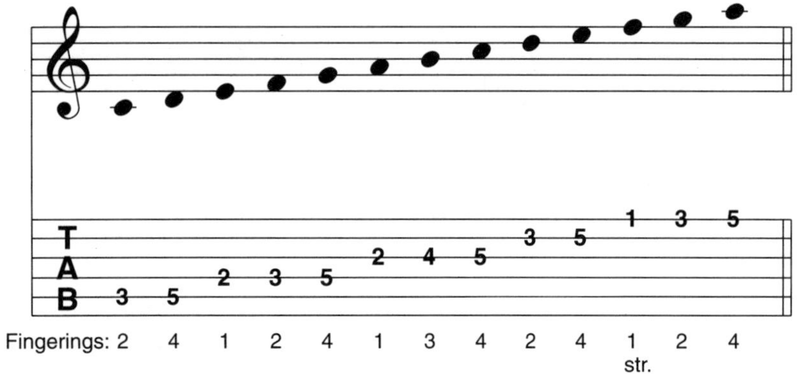

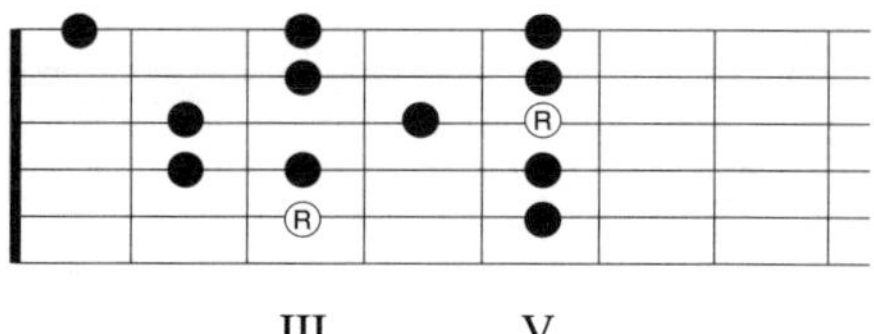

str. = stretch

G Major 2/6

EXAMPLE 6

The fingering of this scale is similar to the C Major scale. It starts with the second finger on the sixth string. This is still in second position, since you are still using your first finger on the second fret. If you wanted to play this fingering starting on a C note, you would have to move up the neck and begin with the C at the eighth fret of the sixth string (seventh position).

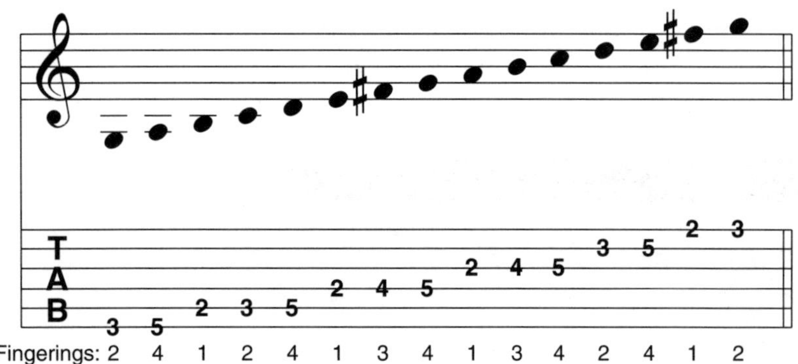

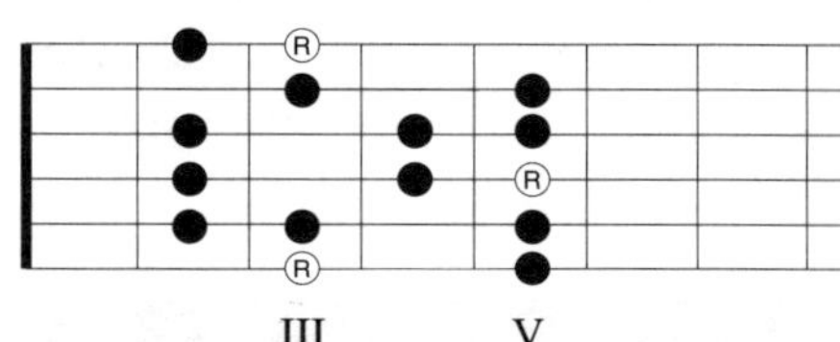

D Major 4/5

EXAMPLE 7

This fingering starts with the fourth finger on the fifth string. Remember: you are still in second position, since your first finger is still on the second fret. You are simply starting on the D note on the fifth fret. If you wanted to play this fingering in the key of C, you would have to move all the way up to the twelfth position and start on the fifth string C with your fourth finger on the fifteenth fret.

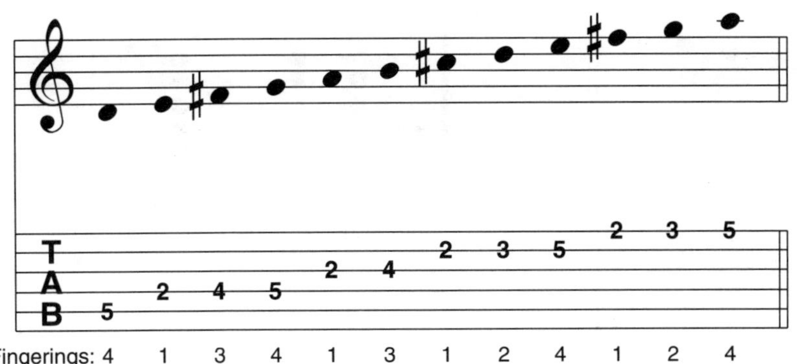

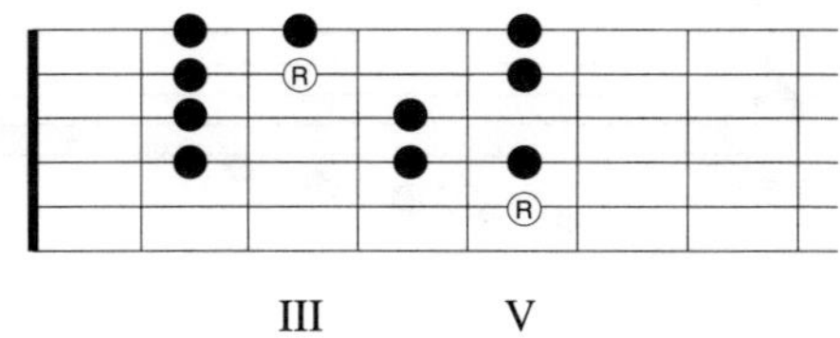

A Major 4/6

EXAMPLE 8

This one starts with your fourth finger on the sixth string. You are still in second position! Don't miss the stretch to the G# note on the fourth string. Just reach out one more fret with your fourth finger without moving your hand from second position. If you want to play this fingering in the key of C, you have to move to the fifth position and start on the sixth string C with your fourth finger on the eighth fret.

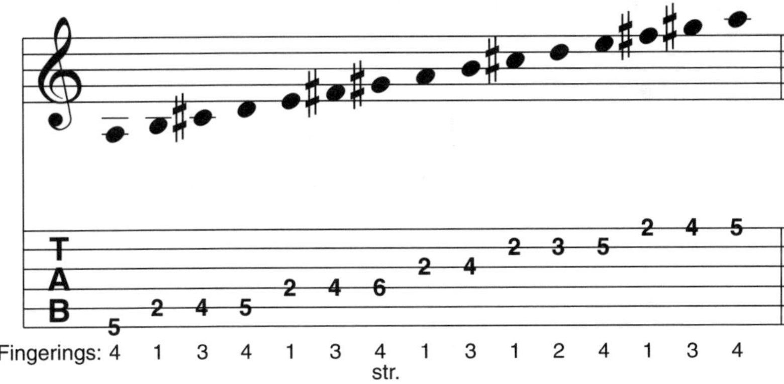

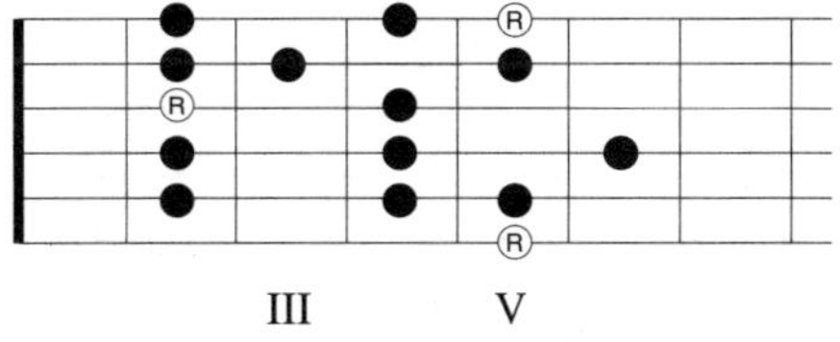

F Major 1/6

EXAMPLE 9

This fingering of the major scale is tricky because of the stretches. Remember, you are still in second position. Don't move your hand down into first position to get the F and B♭ notes. Stretch that first finger out. The more you work with it, the easier it will become. If you want to play this fingering in C, start on the sixth string C at the eighth fret and then proceed in the ninth positon.

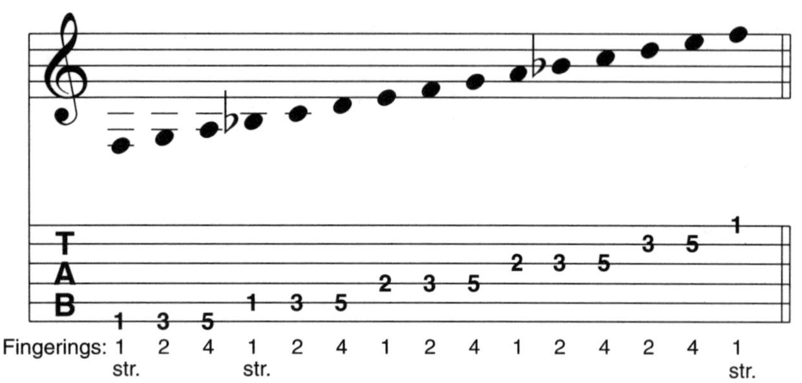

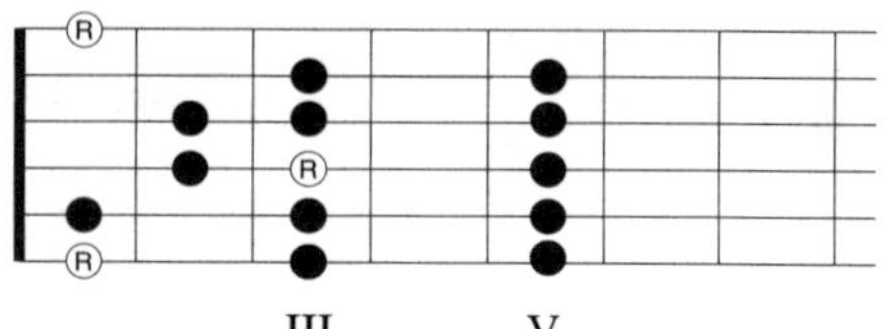

B♭ Major 1/5

EXAMPLE 10

This final fingering for the major scale has a shift from second to third position right in the middle of it! Again, stay in the second position at the beginning and stretch out the first finger to grab the B♭ and E♭. You actually change position, or *shift*, when your first finger plays the D note on the second string, third fret. Practice the shift slowly until you get it. If you want to play this fingering in the key of C, start on fifth string C with your first finger on the third fret, then proceed in the fourth position until it's time to shift to fifth position on the second string.

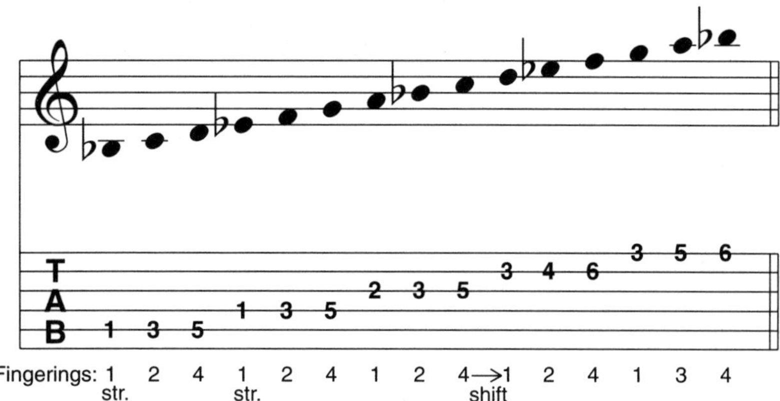

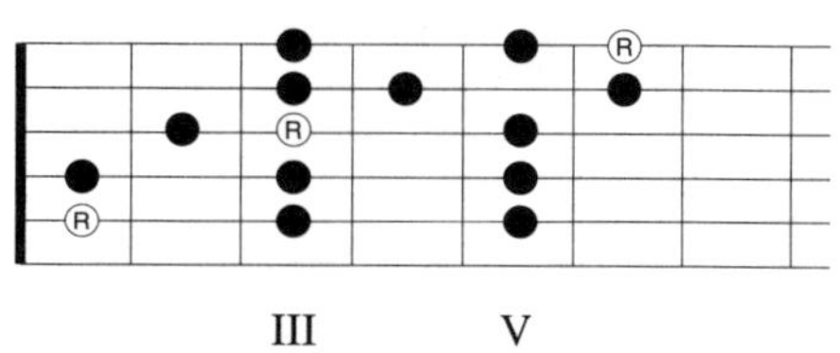

→= Shift

NATURAL MINOR

Minor scales are derived from the major scale. In other words, you can create any minor scale by adjusting notes of the major scale. One of the most common minor scales is the natural minor scale. To build this scale, you lower the third, sixth, and seventh scale degrees of the major scale by a half-step. A minor scale derived in this way is called *parallel minor*, because it has the same root as the major scale.

C Major scale	C	D	E	F	G	A	B	C
	1	2	3	4	5	6	7	8
C Natural Minor scale	C	D	E♭	F	G	A♭	B♭	C
	1	2	♭3	4	5	♭6	♭7	8

The natural minor scale can also be a *relative minor* scale. This is because it is related to a major scale with a different root. The root of a relative minor scale is the sixth degree of its relative major scale. C is the sixth degree of an E♭ Major scale, so C Natural Minor is the relative minor scale to the key of E♭ Major.

E♭ Major scale	E♭	F	G	A♭	B♭	C	D	E♭					
C Natural Minor scale						C	D	E♭	F	G	A♭	B♭	C

So, you can derive C Natural Minor as the parallel minor from C Major, or as the relative minor from E♭ Major. Here is a fingering you can use to play over the chord progression that follows.

C Natural Minor fingering

EXAMPLE 11

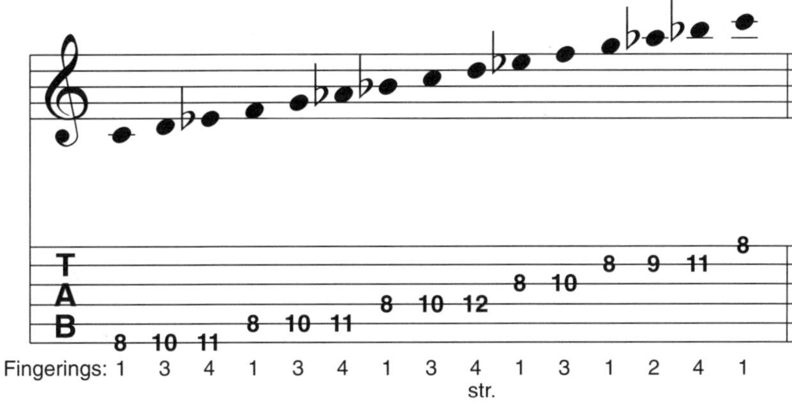

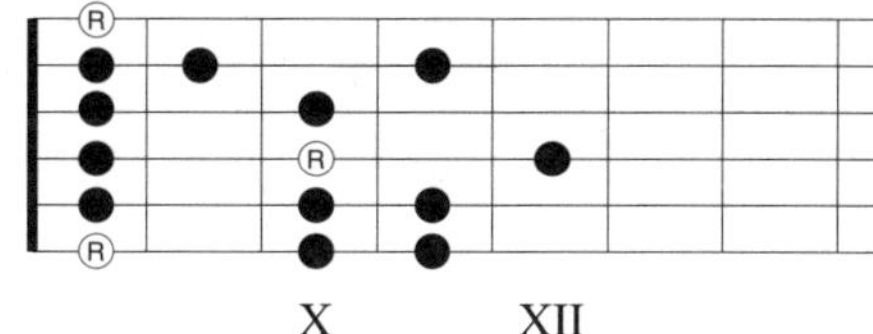

C Natural Minor chord progression

EXAMPLE 12

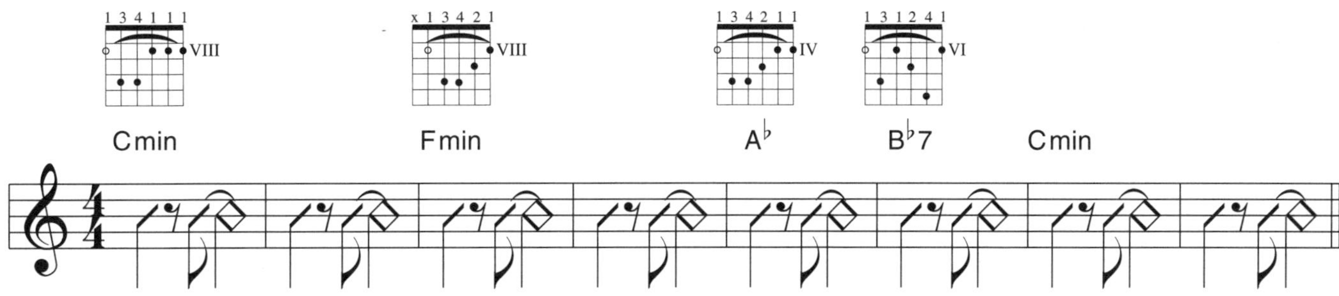

THE DORIAN MODE

The Dorian mode is a minor scale derived by lowering the third and the seventh scale degrees of any major scale.

C Major scale	C	D	E	F	G	A	B	C
	1	2	3	4	5	6	7	8
C Dorian mode	C	D	E♭	F	G	A	B♭	C
	1	2	♭3	4	5	6	♭7	8

It can also be looked at as the scale that results from starting on the second note of any major scale. For instance, if you play a B♭ Major scale, but start on C, you are playing the C Dorian mode.

B♭ Major scale	B♭	C	D	E♭	F	G	A	B♭	
C Dorian mode		C	D	E♭	F	G	A	B♭	C

A common fingering for the C Dorian mode

EXAMPLE 13

You can practice playing this over the chord progression that follows.

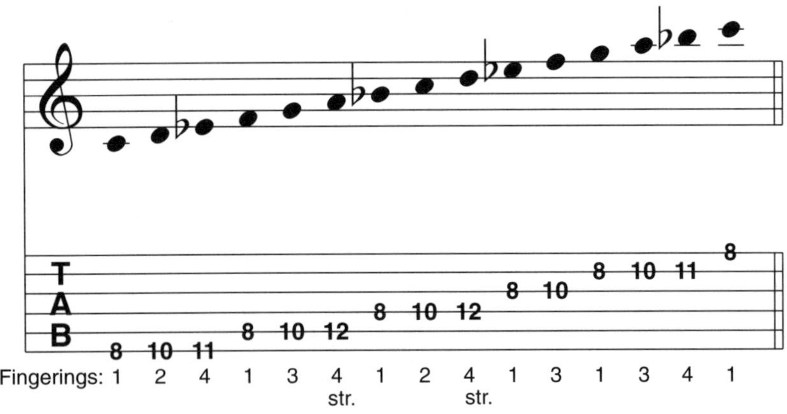

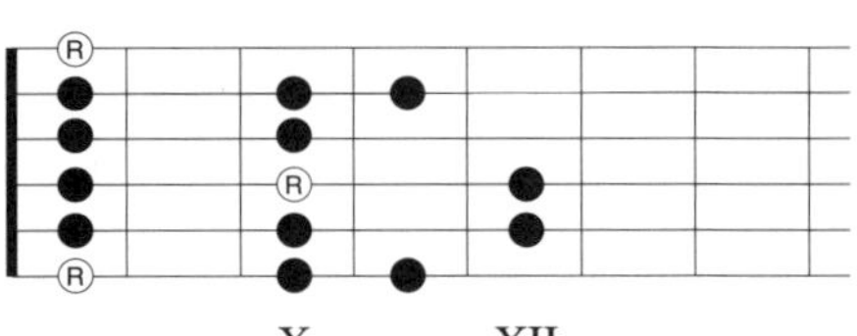

A typical Dorian progression

EXAMPLE 14

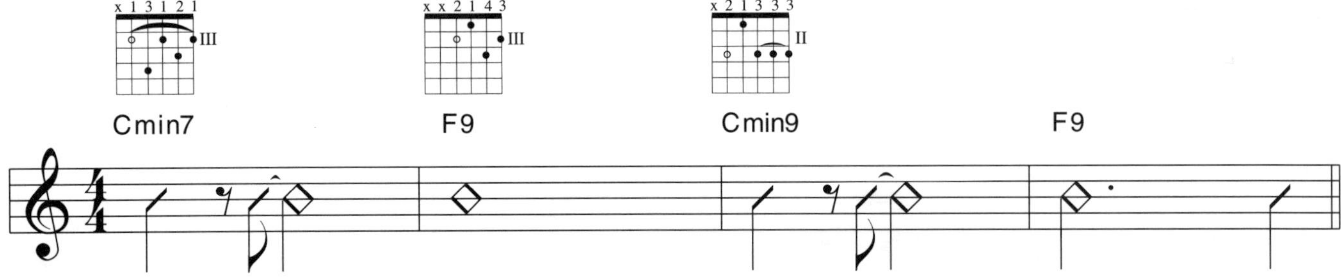

By the way, both Carlos Santana and Pat Martino (a great jazz player!) use the Dorian mode a lot. Check them out and listen for that Dorian sound.

TRIADS

A *triad* is a three-note chord built with the first, third and fifth scale degrees. There are four different types of triads:

Triad type	Scale degrees		
Major (Maj)	1	3	5
Minor (min)	1	♭3	5
Diminished (dim)	1	♭3	♭5
Augmented (aug)	1	3	♯5

INVERSIONS

Each type of triad can be played three different ways depending on which of the three notes is on the bottom of the triad.

If the **root** is on the bottom, the triad is in **root position.**
If the **3rd** is on the bottom, the triad is in **first inversion.**
If the **5th** is on the bottom, the triad is in **second inversion.**

EXAMPLE 15

This example shows the triads in their inversions. Play them across the page from left to right so you can listen to how the inversions sound. Then play them down the page from top to bottom so you can focus on the different quality of each type of triad.

Root Position | 1st inversion | 2nd inversion

Maj

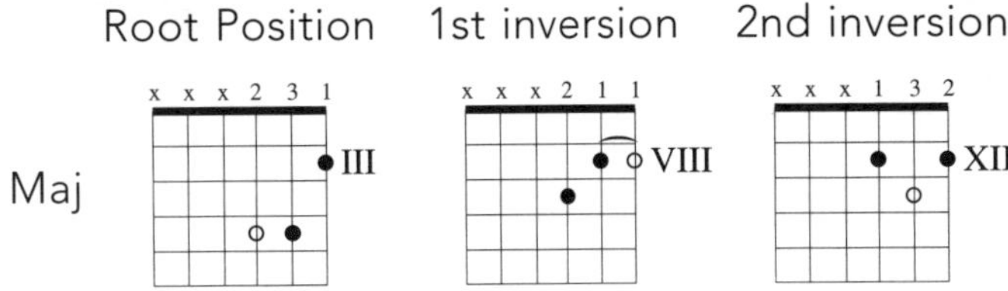

min

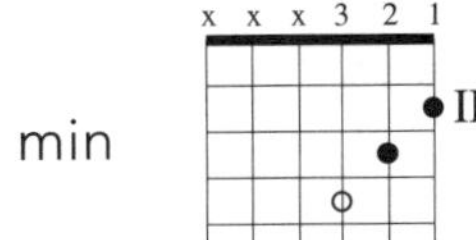

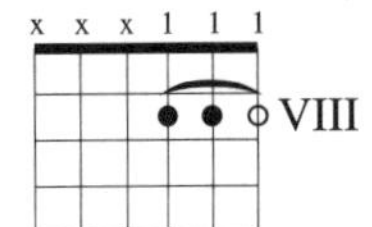

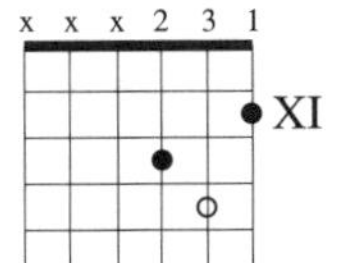

dim

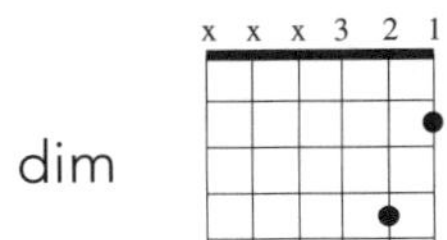

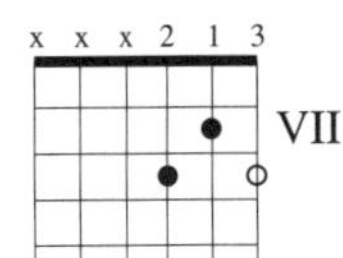

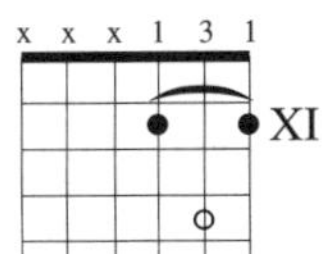

aug

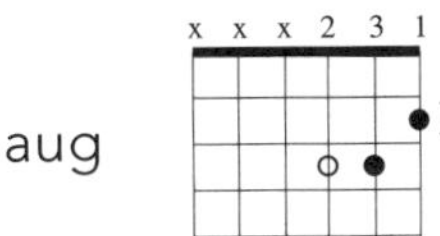

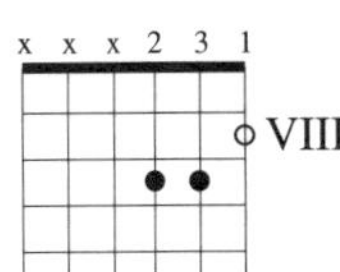

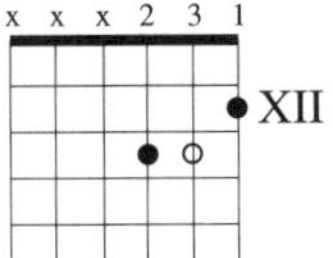

PHOTO\COURTESY OF MUSE RECORDS

Pat Martino

DIATONIC TRIADS

Diatonic triads are the triads that are directly related to a particular key. The notes used to make up each diatonic triad are taken from the major scale of the key, and the quality of each triad is the same in every key. Triads are built in 3rds on each note of the major scale. These triads are the harmonies for that key.

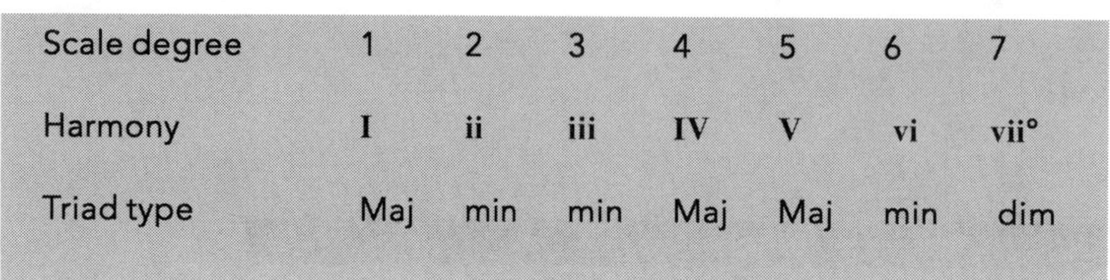

Scale degree	1	2	3	4	5	6	7
Harmony	I	ii	iii	IV	V	vi	vii°
Triad type	Maj	min	min	Maj	Maj	min	dim

Notice that upper case Roman numerals are used for major harmonies, and that lower case Roman numerals are used for minor and diminished harmonies.

C Major diatonic triads

EXAMPLE 16

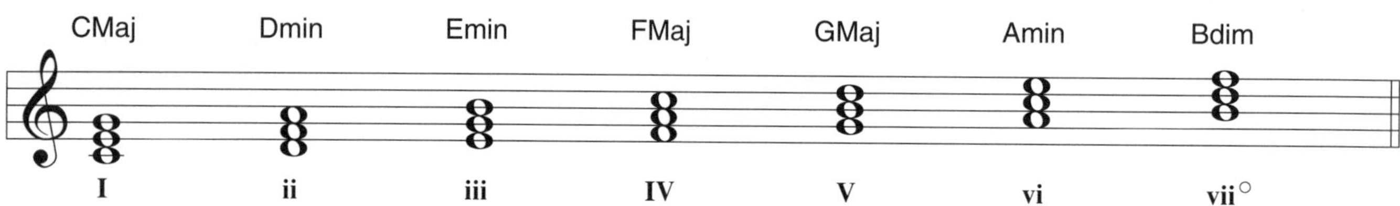

The following fingerings show the diatonic triads in C going up the neck from the first position to the twelfth position on the top three strings. Here is a hint to help you: from the Dmin triad on up, keep your third finger on the neck at all times. This is your *guide finger* and will help you to move smoothly from one fingering to another.

EXAMPLE 17

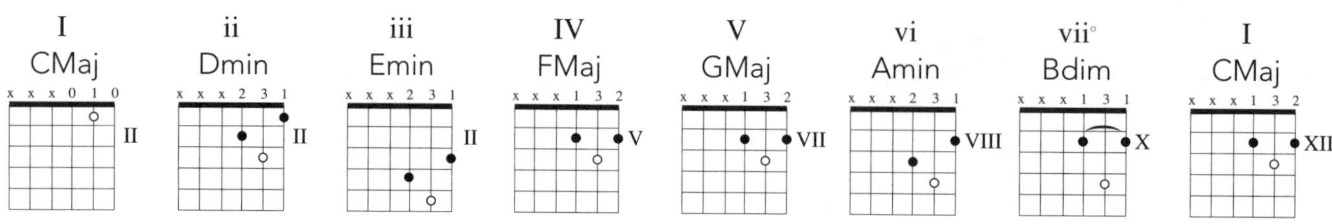

SEVENTH CHORDS

A lot of the harmony in jazz is more complex sounding than simple triads. Often, these chords have four or more notes in them. The first group of these complex chords we will look at are called 7th chords.

To build a 7th chord, you simply add a major or minor 3rd above the 5th of each triad. This note will be a 7th above the root of the triad.

MAJOR 7TH

The Major 7th chord

Add a major 3rd above the 5th to make a major 7th chord, which is written Maj7. The 5th of a C Major chord is the note G. Add a 3rd above the G note, and you get the note B.

CMaj7	C	E	G	B
	1	3	5	7

The following diagram shows how this works. It also shows a CMaj7 *arpeggio*. An arpeggio, or broken chord, is a very common way to play a chord, and is one of the important building blocks of a good jazz guitar solo. Practice playing all the arpeggios that follow, and be ready to use them when you improvise!

EXAMPLE 18

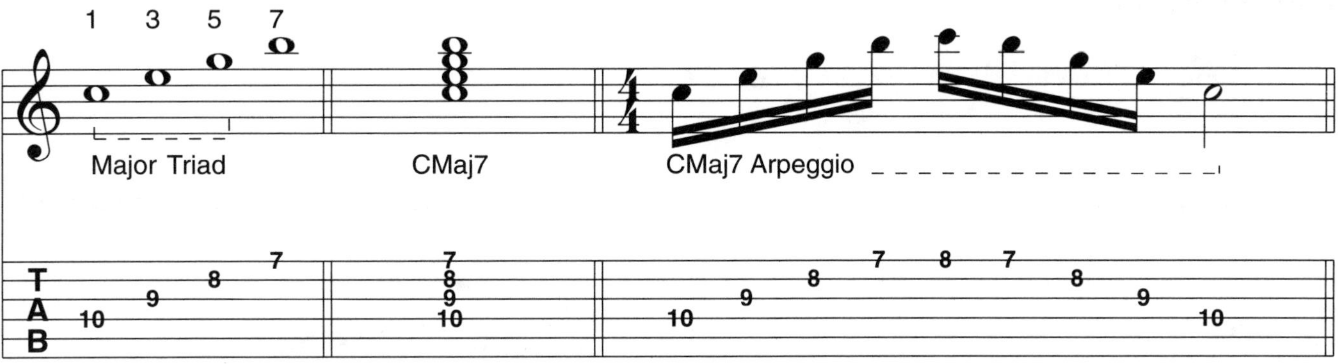

DOMINANT 7TH

To build a dominant 7th chord, you add a minor 3rd on top of a major triad. The distance of this note from the root is a minor 7th. You do not have to write C dominant 7 when you write out the chord. It is accepted short hand to simply write *C7*, and everyone will know what you mean.

A minor 3rd above the note G is a B♭. B♭ is a minor 7th above C, the root of the chord.

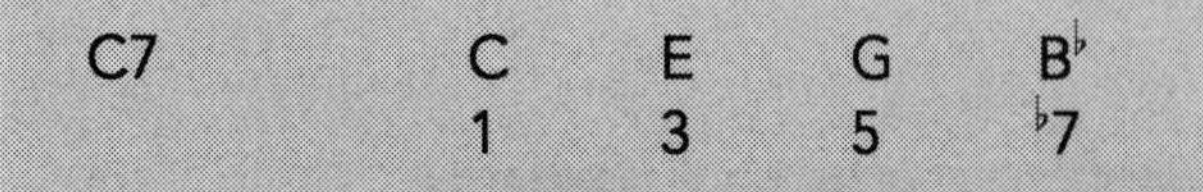

C7	C	E	G	B♭
	1	3	5	♭7

EXAMPLE 19

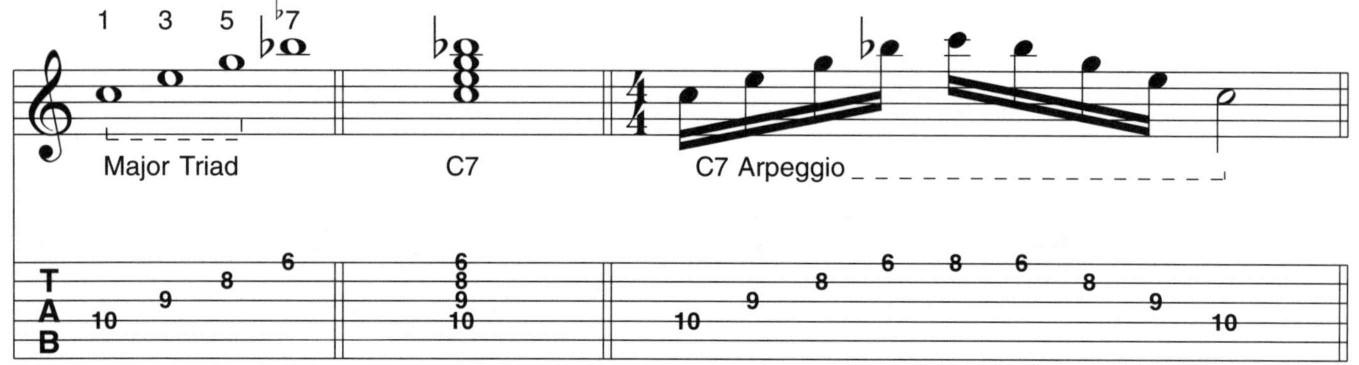

MINOR 7TH

To make a Minor 7th chord, written *min7*, you add a minor 3rd to a minor triad, and the distance from this note to the root is a minor 7th.

Cmin7	C	E♭	G	B♭
	1	♭3	5	♭7

EXAMPLE 20

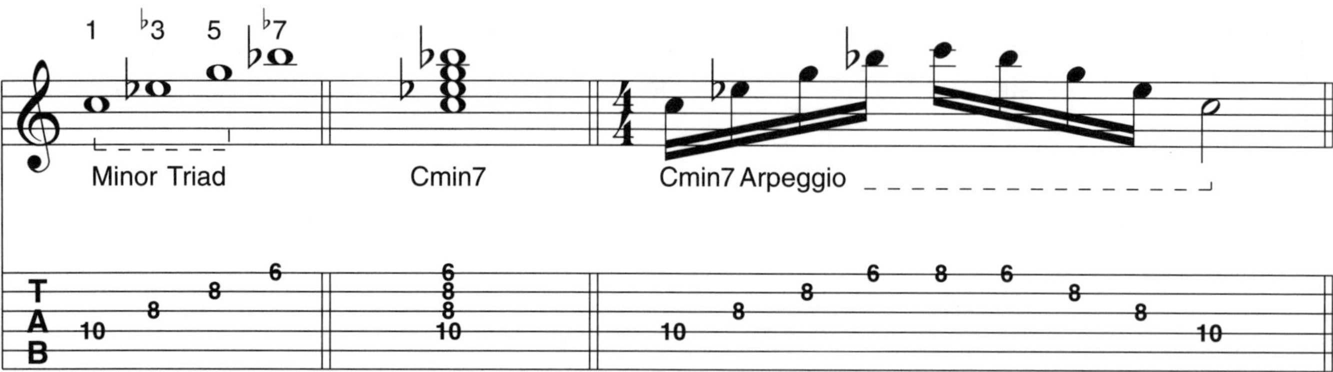

MINOR 7♭5

To build a minor 7♭5 chord, written *min7♭5*, you add a major 3rd to a diminished triad. The distance from this note to the root is a minor 7th.

Cmin7♭5	C	E♭	G♭	B♭
	1	♭3	♭5	♭7

EXAMPLE 21

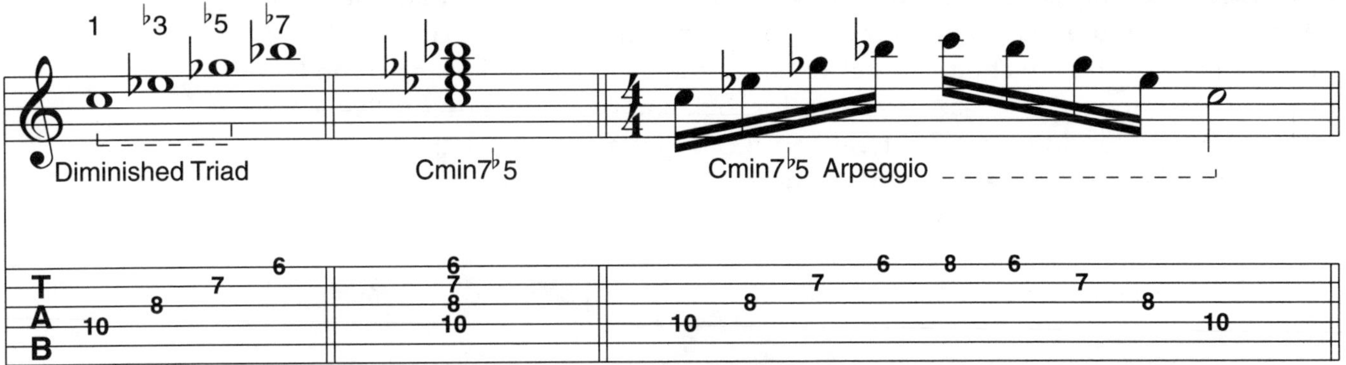

DIMINISHED 7TH

And finally, to build a diminished 7 chord, written *dim7*, add a minor 3rd to a diminished triad. The distance from this note to the root is a diminished 7th, which is enharmonically equivalent to a major 6th.

Cdim7	C	E♭	G♭	B♭♭ (A)
	1	♭3	♭5	♭♭7 (6)

EXAMPLE 22

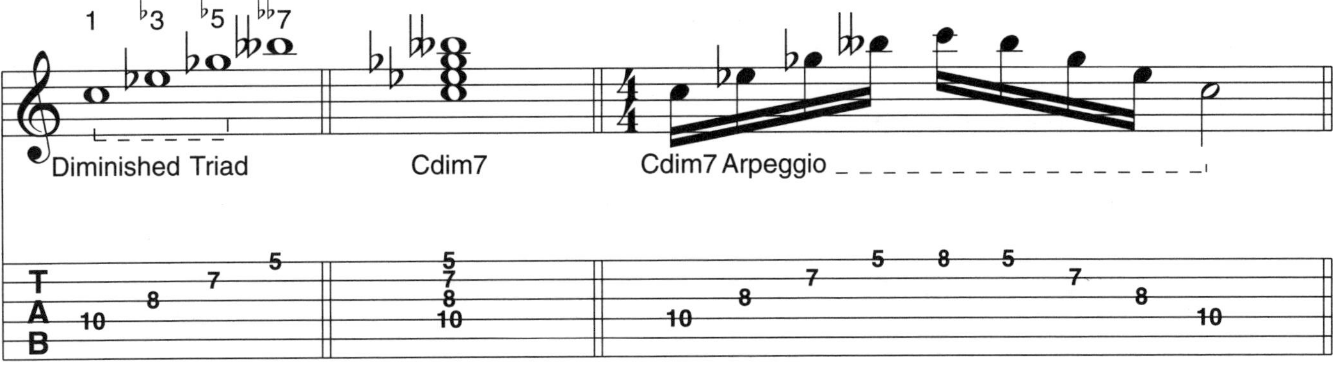

DIATONIC 7TH CHORDS

If we add another 3rd above each one of the diatonic triads, we will have diatonic 7th chords. These are all four-note 7th chords, but they vary in type according to the intervals that result from stacking 3rds on each note of the scale. The best thing is that the quality of these 7th chords remains the same no matter what key you are in.

These chords define the harmony of the key. In other words, if you are in the key of C, there are only seven possible 7th chords that you can use. Each of these has a function in the major key. If there is a chord in the song that doesn't fit the profile of any of the 7th chords in the key of C, then you are no longer in the key of C! This is more true for jazz than it is for rock and blues, where it is likely, for instance, to find a dominant 7th type chord being played on a I chord, or a IV chord, as well as the more "correct" V chord. See page 19 for a more thorough explanation of *functional harmony*.

SCALE DEGREE	1	2	3	4	5	6	7
HARMONY	I	ii	iii	IV	V	vi	vii
7th CHORD	Maj7	min7	min7	Maj7	Dom7	min7	min7♭5

DIATONIC 7TH CHORD FINGERINGS

Diatonic 7th Chords in C — EXAMPLE 23

The following diagram shows the diatonic 7th chords in C using the fifth, fourth, third, and second strings. The notes in the parentheses on the first string are optional. Once you learn these fingerings, and the fingerings that follow for F Major, you will be able to play the diatonic 7th chords in any key, and on two different string sets. You just have to know where the roots are on the fifth string and sixth string. In the fingerings given here for C Major, the chords are all in root position with the roots on the fifth string.

Play the sequence from left to right, starting on CMaj7 and ending on Bmin7♭5.

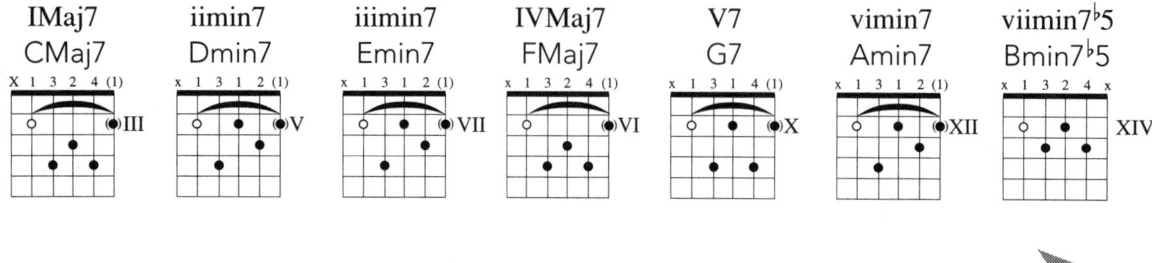

Diatonic 7th Chords in F

EXAMPLE 24

The following diagram shows the diatonic 7th chord fingerings in the key of F using the sixth, fourth, third and second strings. In this set of fingerings the chords are all in root position, with the roots on the sixth string. You should mute out the fifth string with the fat part of your first or second finger—whichever one plays the note on the sixth string.

Play the sequence from left to right, starting on FMaj7 and ending on Emin7♭5.

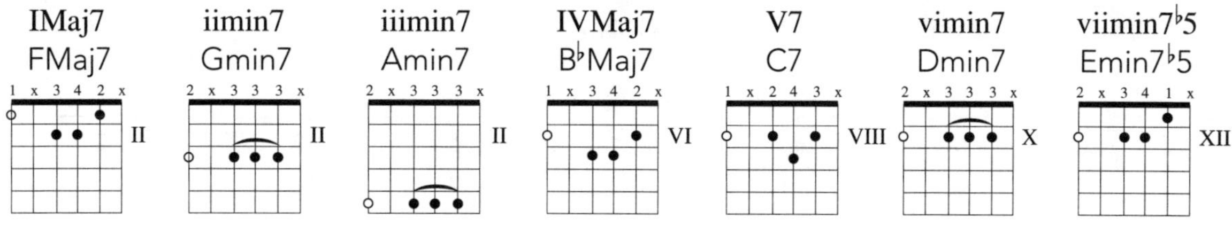

FUNCTIONAL HARMONY

Remember, the sequence of 7th chord types is the same for any key. Just add the letter names to the 7th chord qualities and you've got the chords in that key. This concept is extremely important. In jazz, the tonal center—the note that is the root the key—often changes for a period of time. There are a lot of tunes that have more than one key center in them. That is usually not true in rock songs.

If the key is changing during a tune, how do you figure out what key you are in at any given time? You can do this by analyzing each of the chord types. Is it a iimin7 chord? Is it a V7 chord? Once you figure out the quality of each chord, it will be apparent what key you are in.

For example, if you are in the key of C and you see a D7 chord, all the alarms ought to go off because the D chord in the key of C is Dmin7, right? The only time a dominant 7 chord appears is as a V7 chord, which in the key of C is a G7 chord. Since D7 must be a V7 chord, (and it is!) then you must be in the key of G at that moment because D7 is V7 in the key of G.

Gmaj7	Amin7	Bmin7	Cmaj7	D7
Imaj7	**iimin7**	**iiimin7**	**IVmaj7**	**V7**

We call this concept *functional harmony* because it is the function of the chord, whether it's a Imaj7 or a iimin7, etc., that is important.

HOW TO USE THE DIATONIC 7TH CHORDS

Now that you've learned two fingerings for the Diatonic 7th chords, let's put them to use. The chord progression in Examples 25 and 26 is very similar to the opening section in Van Morrison's "*Moondance.*" The progression is: Amin7, Bmin7, CMaj7, Bmin7.

EXAMPLE 25

Here is the chord progression using the diatonic 7th chord shapes with the root on the sixth string.

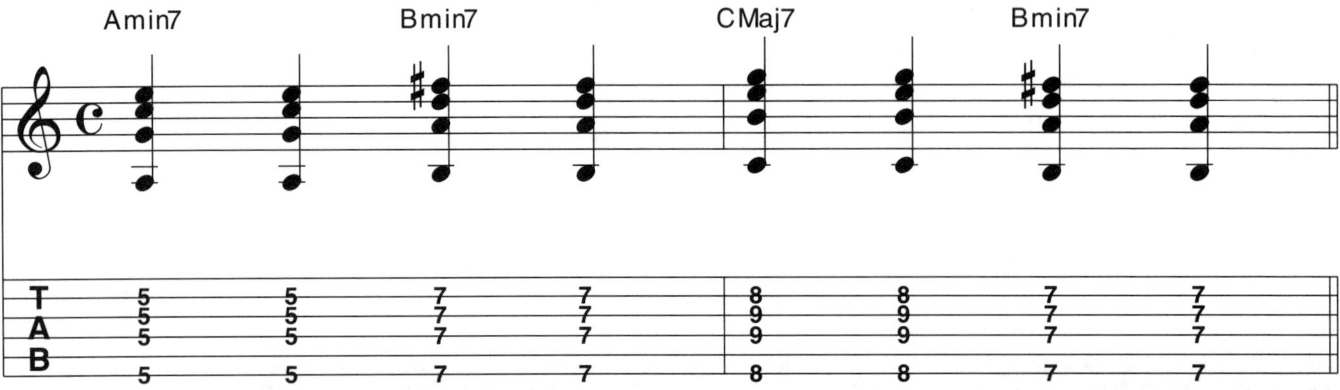

EXAMPLE 26

This is the same chord progression with the roots of the diatonic 7th chords on the fifth string.

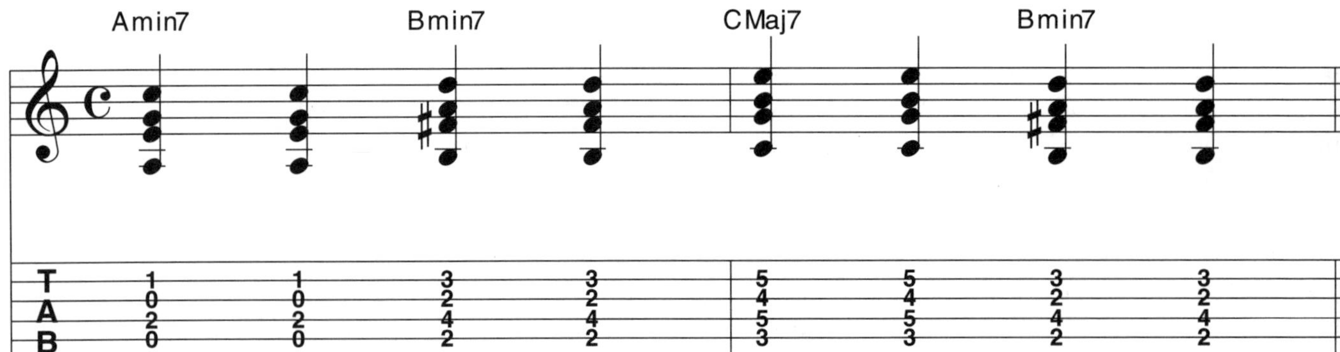

DIATONIC 7TH ARPEGGIOS

Another good way to memorize the diatonic 7th chords is to arpeggiate them, both ascending and descending. Each arpeggio in the following example is one octave, and all are confined to the top three strings. This is where they are easiest to hear, and they move up the neck on the top three strings, which is where you probably play most of the time when soloing.

EXAMPLE 27

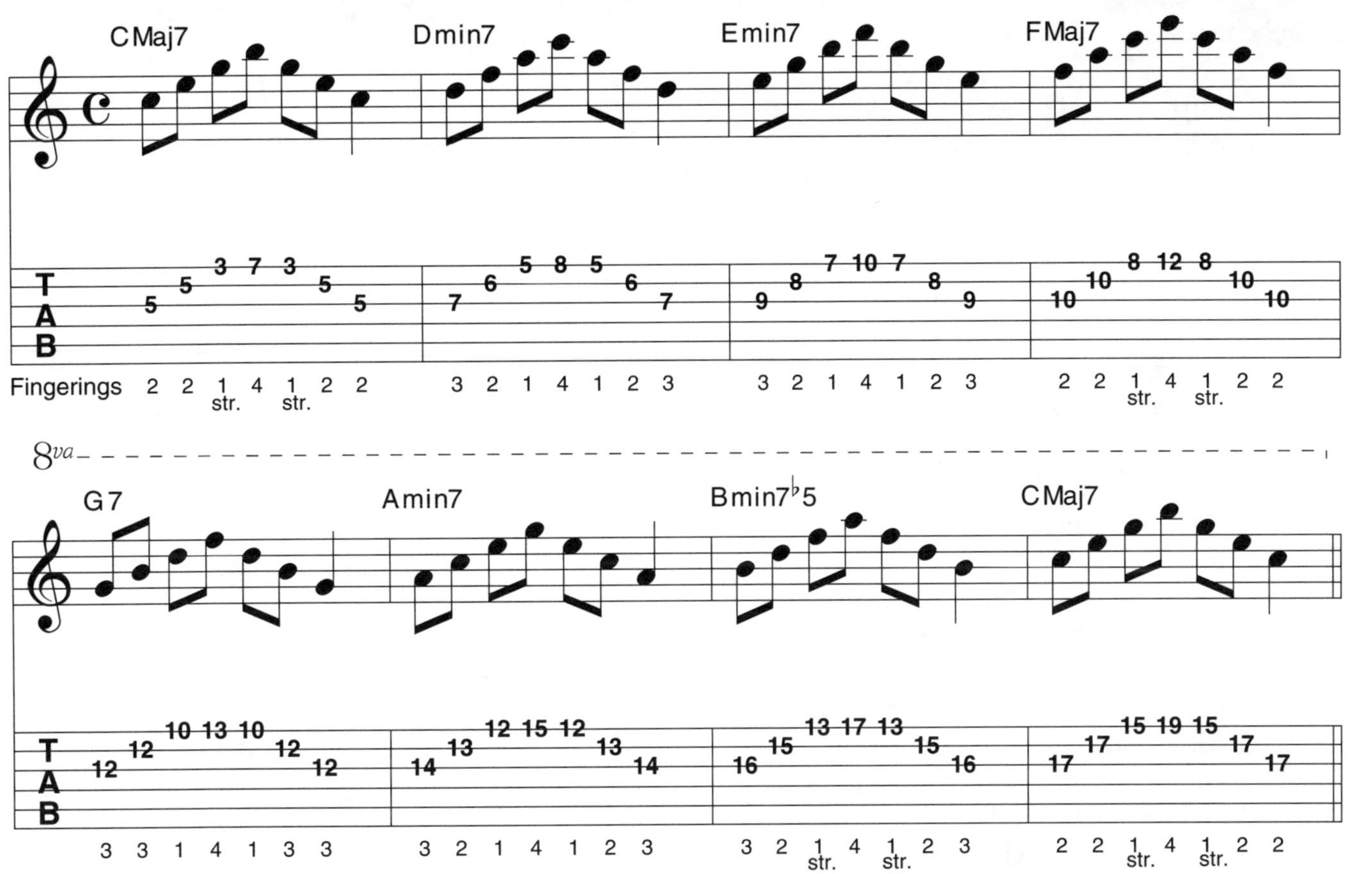

PHOTO • INSTITUTE OF JAZZ STUDIES

Joe Pass

MORE COMPLEX CHORDS AND SUBSTITUTIONS

MAJOR 9TH

What is a 9th chord? Good question! Simply put, to make a 9th chord, you add the 9th scale degree, which is a 2nd plus an octave, above the root of an already existing 7th chord or triad. If we added a 9th to a CMaj7 chord, we would get a *CMaj9* chord.

CMaj7	C	E	G	B	
CMaj9	C	E	G	B	D
	1	3	5	7	9

Remember, 9 is the same as 2, but an octave higher.

C	D	E	F	G	A	B	C	D
1	2	3	4	5	6	7	8	9

Why do it? The Maj9 chord has more "color" than a Maj7 chord. That doesn't make it better, only different.

MAJOR 9TH SUBSTITUTIONS

A Maj9 can be used as a subtitute for a Maj7 chord. In fact, here is a cool trick that you should know: when you see a CMaj7 chord (or any IMaj7 chord), you can play Emin7 (iiimin7). Why? An Emin7 chord has exactly the same notes as the CMaj9, minus the C.

CMaj7	C	E	G	B	
CMaj9	C	E	G	B	D
Emin7		E	G	B	D

Two voicings for CMaj9

A *voicing* is a way of arranging the notes of a chord on the guitar. Each voicing has its own particular sound.

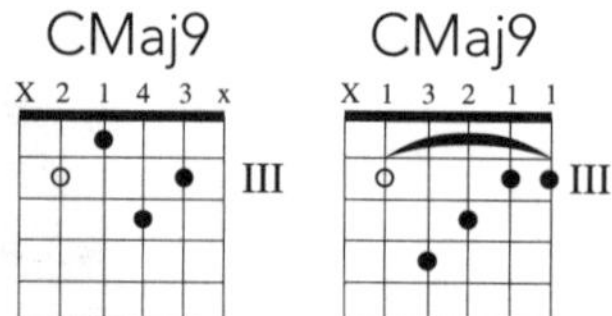

MAJ9 add 13

You can make a CMaj9 chord even more "colorful" by adding a 13th. A 13th is a 6th plus an octave, and the name of this chord would be CMaj13add9.

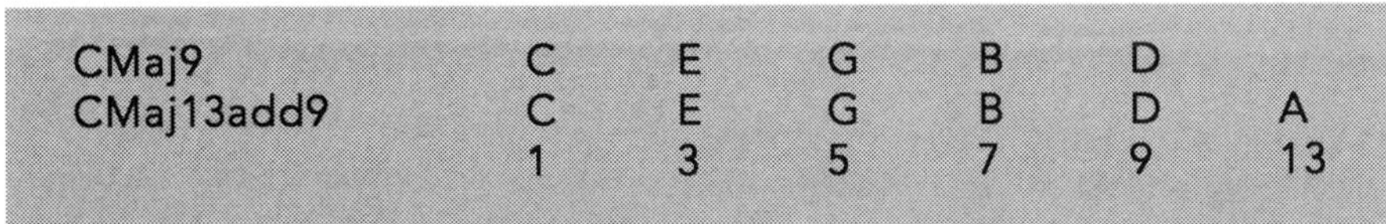

CMaj9	C	E	G	B	D	
CMaj13add9	C	E	G	B	D	A
	1	3	5	7	9	13

MAJ13add9 SUBSTITUTIONS

This can still be substituted for CMaj7!

Two voicings for CMaj13add9

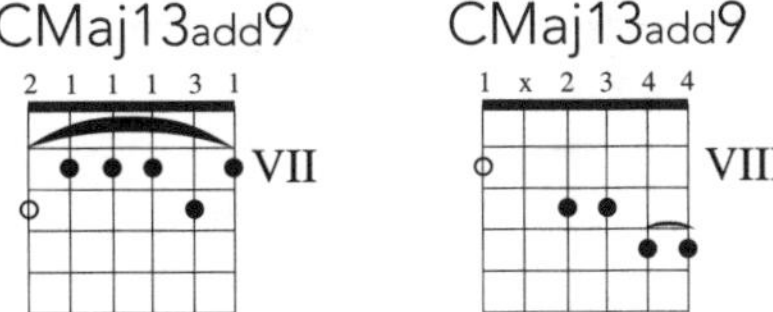

George Benson

PHOTO: GREGORY JACKSON • COURTESY OF WARNERS BROTHERS RECORDS

THE MINOR 9

The *min9* chord is a darkly colorful and sad sounding chord. It can substitute for a minor triad or a min7 chord, and it works best as either a **imin9** chord or as a **vimin9** chord. Theoretically, you build a min9 chord by adding a 9th to a min7 chord.

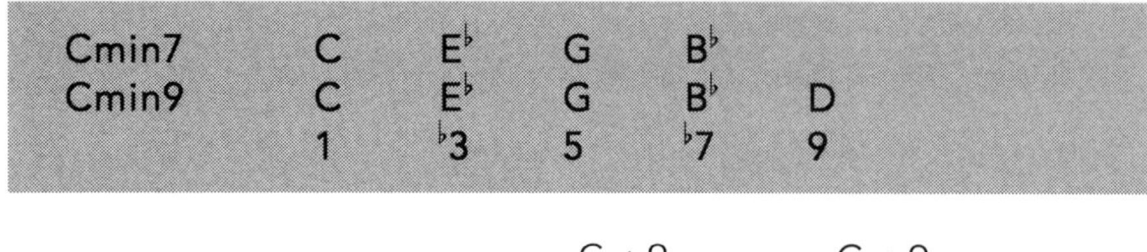

Cmin7	C	E♭	G	B♭	
Cmin9	C	E♭	G	B♭	D
	1	♭3	5	♭7	9

Two voicings for Cmin9

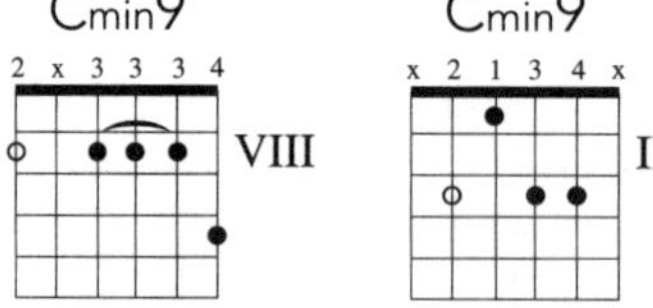

There is another way to look at this chord, and that is to add the 9th to a minor triad, and voice it as a 2.

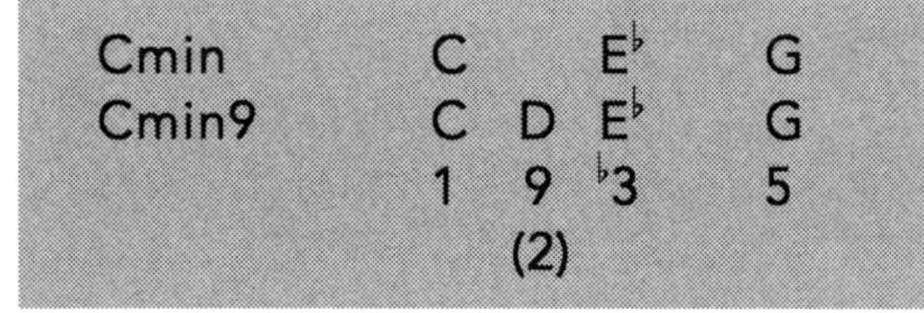

Cmin	C		E♭	G
Cmin9	C	D	E♭	G
	1	9	♭3	5
		(2)		

The character of this chord lies in the fact that the 9th and the ♭3rd are on adjacent strings and so are only a minor 2nd (a half-step) apart. When you hear the following voicings, notice how the 9th and the ♭3rd are almost clashing, yet, when the other notes are present, the whole chord sounds excellently dark!

Two voicings for Emin9

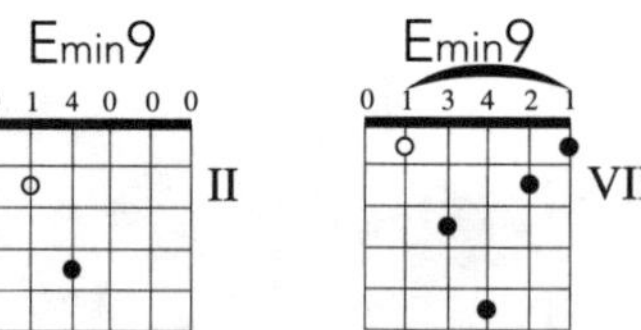

THE add9

If you take the min9 chord and change the ♭3 to a 3, you will have what is called an add9 chord. Or, just add a 9th to a major triad. The 9 is almost always voiced as a 2, which gives this chord its character. Again, the 9 and the 3 are on adjacent strings, and they are only a major 2nd (whole-step) apart.

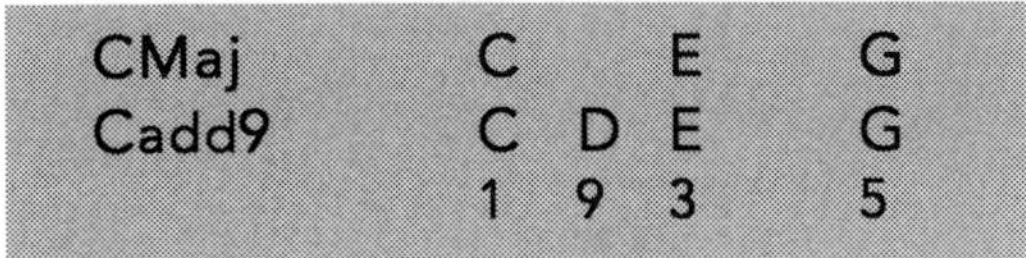

CMaj	C		E	G
Cadd9	C	D	E	G
	1	9	3	5

Add9 SUBSTITUTIONS

You can use add9 chords to substitute for **I** and **IV** chords, and they sound very beautiful, lush and full.

Two voicings for Eadd9

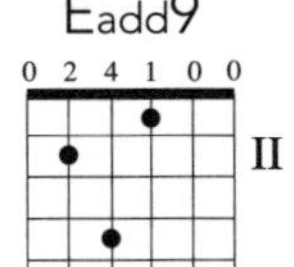

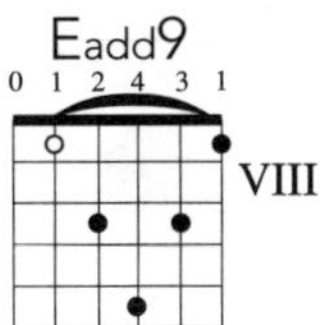

Three voicings for Aadd9

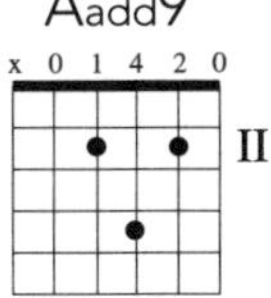

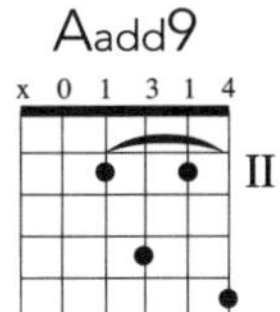

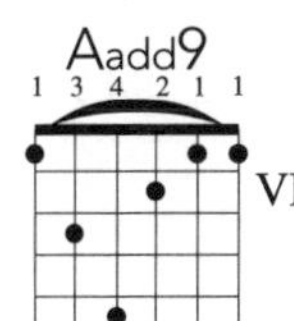

THE DOMINANT 9TH

This is the chord you've heard in all those funky James Brown tunes! And in the blues, too. You make this chord by adding a 9th to a dominant 7th chord.

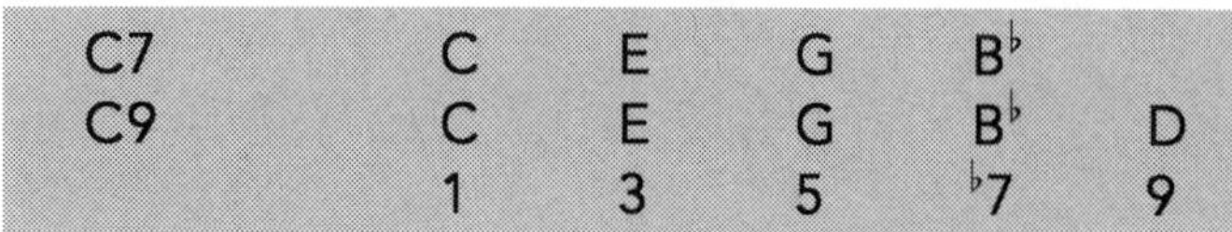

C7	C	E	G	B♭	
C9	C	E	G	B♭	D
	1	3	5	♭7	9

Here is the most common voicing for the dominant 9th chord:

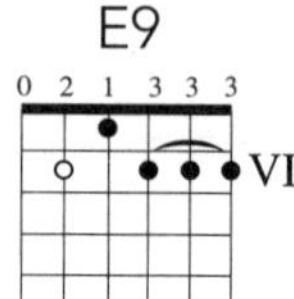

EXAMPLE 28

A cool trick with this chord is to slide the top three notes (the ones you are barring with your 3rd finger) two frets up and then back down to the starting position. You've heard it before and it sounds so slick!

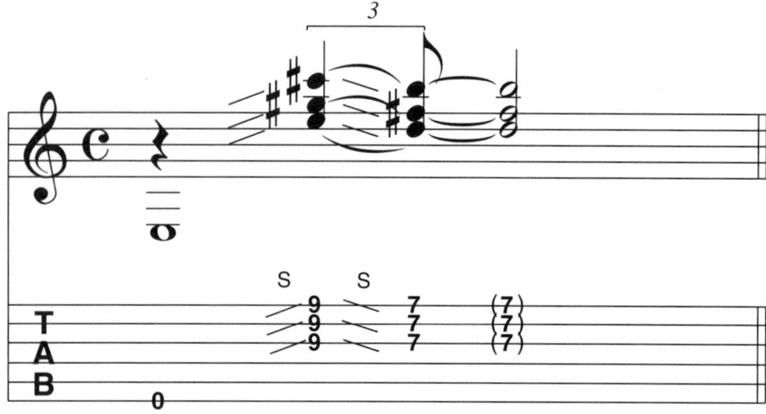

Here is another voicing for the dominant 9th chord:

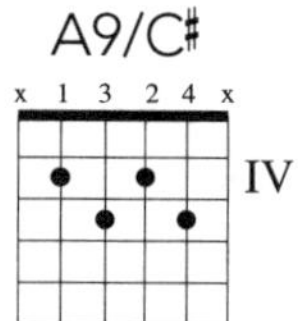

EXAMPLE 29

You can use the same sliding trick as you did with the other voicing of E9 by sliding the notes under your second, third, and fourth fingers up two frets, and then returning to your starting position.

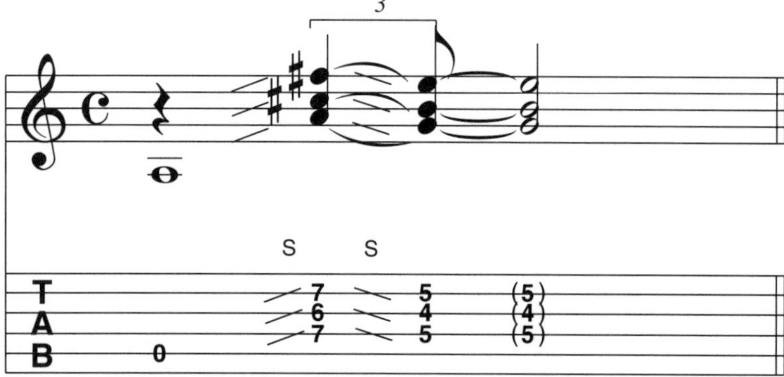

13THS

A 13th chord is built by adding a 13th (a 6th plus an octave) to an already existing 7th chord. The voicings below, however, only have four notes. The notes jazz players usual use are: 1, 3 (or ♭3), 7 (or ♭7) and 13.

MAJ13 CHORDS

CMaj13	C	E	B	A
	1	3	7	13

Maj13 Chord Substitutions: CMaj13 can substitute for CMaj7 or CMaj9 or just plain C!

A voicing for CMaj13

CMaj13

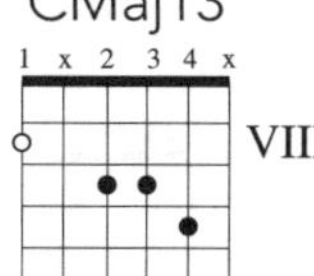

13 CHORDS

C13	C	E	B♭	A
	1	3	♭7	13

13 Chord Substitutions: A 13 chord can substitute for a 7th or a 9th chord.

Two voicings for C13

C13

C13

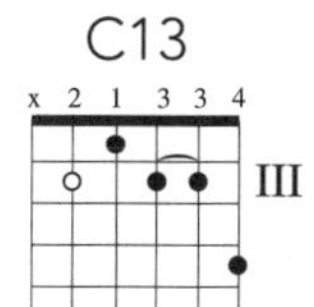

MIN13 CHORDS

Cminl3	C	E♭	B♭	A
	1	♭3	♭7	13

Min13 Chord Substitutions: A min13 chord can substitute for a min7 or, sometimes, a min9. Use this one sparingly! It has a very unusual sound!

Two voicings for Cmin13

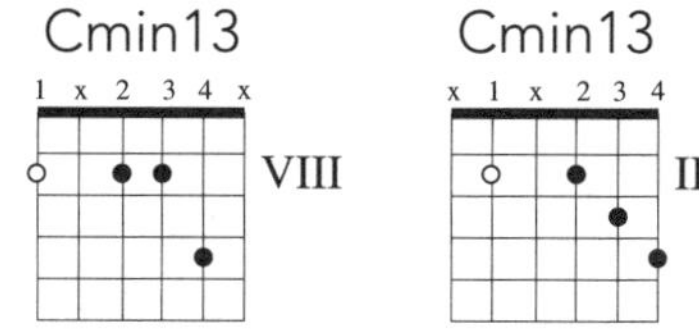

You may have to take some time to get familiar with the sound of this chord, since it sounds a little "out."

ALTERED DOMINANT 7THS

Altered dominant 7th chords are 7th, 9th, and 13th chords where the 5th and/or the 9th scale degrees have been raised or lowered by a half-step. There are a lot of possibilities and combinations here, so we are just going to look at three of them.

7♯9 CHORDS

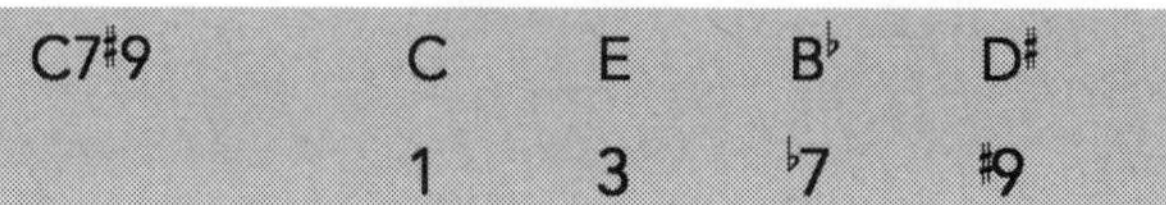

C7♯9	C	E	B♭	D♯
	1	3	♭7	♯9

This notorious chord has earned a nick-name: "*the Hendrix Chord*!" Ah! you know it! What's cool is that it has both a 3 and a ♭3. A ♯9 is a ♯2 plus an octave, which is enharmonically equal to a ♭3.

A voicing for C7♯9

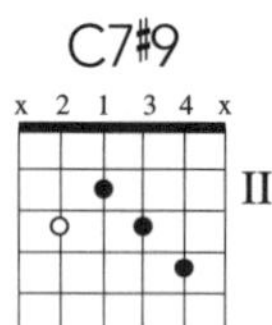

7♭9 CHORDS

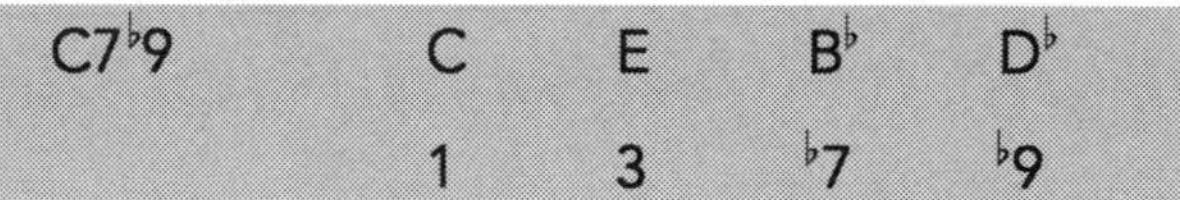

C7♭9	C	E	B♭	D♭
	1	3	♭7	♭9

The 7♭9 chord is often used for a V7♭9 when going to a imin. Also, it is often used in conjunction with a 7♯9. For example, here is a common V7— imin change:

C7♯9 to C7♭9	to	Fmin9
V7	to	imin

A voicing for C7♭9

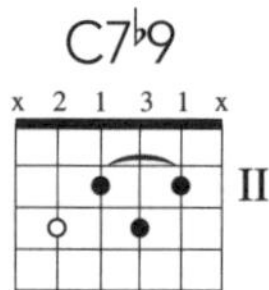

AUG7 CHORDS

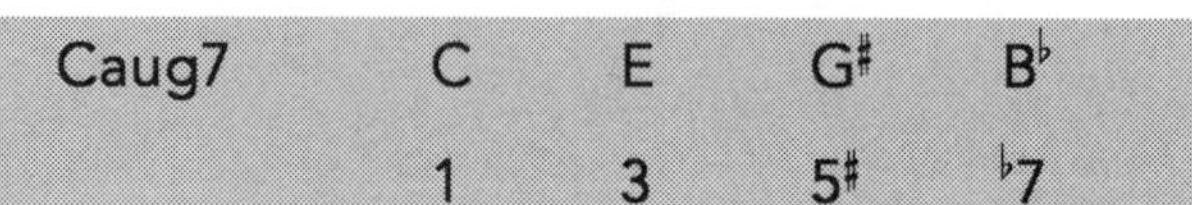

Caug7	C	E	G♯	B♭
	1	3	5♯	♭7

Augmented 7th chords are often written as +7. This doesn't mean that you augment the 7! This chord is simply a dominant 7th chord with a raised 5th (the 5th is raised one half-step). It is a great chord to use when moving back to I.

A voicing for Caug7

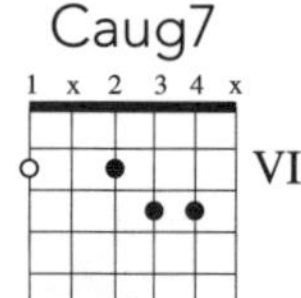

SLASH CHORDS

You may have seen complicated looking chords such as: FMaj7/G. Right? What do they mean when they put that slash (/) in there? The concept is to play the chord over a bass note other than the root. So, FMaj7/G means to play an FMaj7 chord with the note G in the bass. You can describe this as "FMaj7 with a G in the bass."

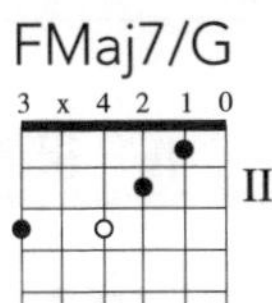

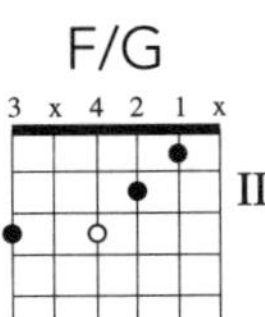

Another common chord/bass note combination is the simpler F/G, which is moveable all over the neck. In the key of C, you use this chord as a substitute for the V7 chord because the G in the bass and the F note in the chord make your ears want to hear C, just like a V7 chord does.

You will often see chords like C/F. These are written this way in order to get a particular sound or voicing. For instance, the notes of a C/F chord are the same as FMaj9, but what is really wanted is a C Major triad with an F in the bass.

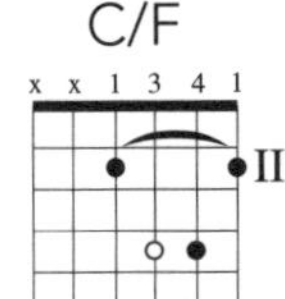

FMaj9	F	A	C	E	G
C/F	F		C	E	G

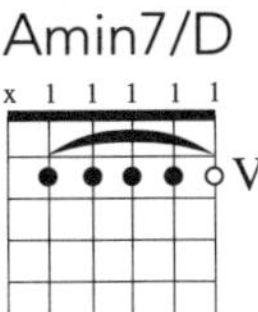

Finally, you will see chords like Amin7/D, which is also a substitute for a V7 chord in the key of G. It is the iimin7 chord with the root of the V chord in the bass, and it wants to go to I, in this case, G. It is very closely related to the V9 chord.

D9	D	F♯	A	C	E	
Amin7/D	D		A	C	E	G

JAZZ CHORD PROGRESSIONS AND LICKS

USING SUBSTITUTIONS

It's high time we put some of these fancy jazz chords into practice! We can use the 9th, 13th, and altered dominant 7th chords as substitutions for the basic rock chords to make a typical rock progression sound a whole lot hipper and jazzier. Let's look at a basic rock progression: Amin7—D7—E7. In this first example, we have made the following substitutions:

Amin9	for	Amin7
D9	for	D7
E7#9	for	E7

EXAMPLE 30

Remember to follow the indicated rhythms.

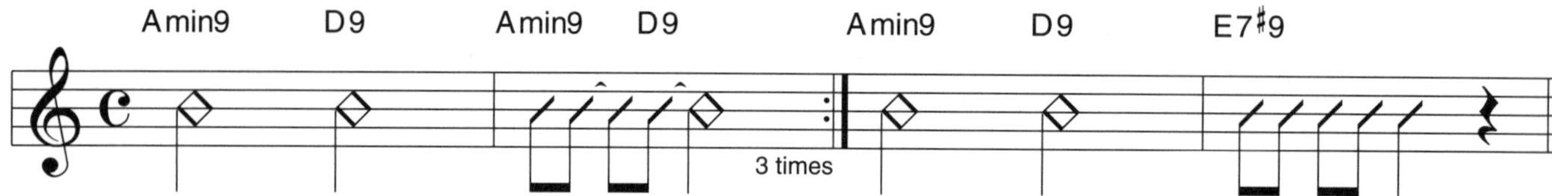

In Example 31 we will make these substitutions:

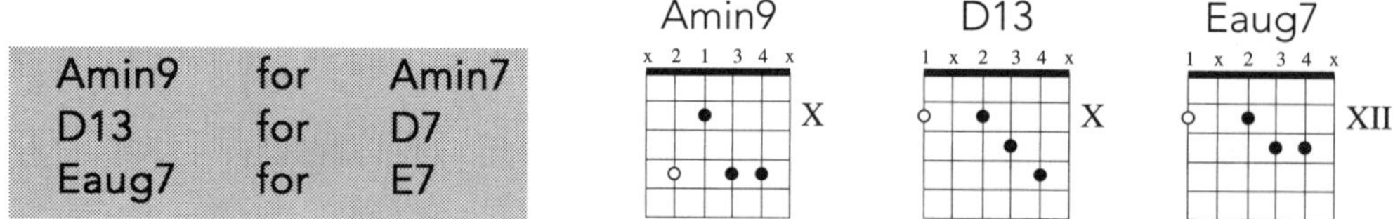

Amin9	for	Amin7
D13	for	D7
Eaug7	for	E7

EXAMPLE 31

Again, pay attention to the rhythms and listen to how these chords really make the progression sound jazzy!

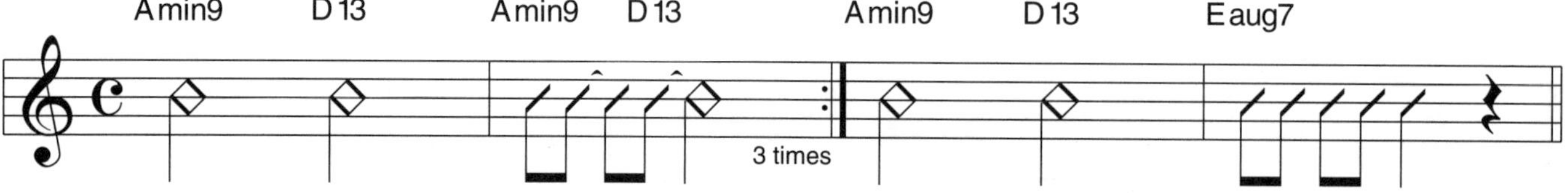

JAZZ CHORDS AND MELODY

One of the things you need to know about jazz chords is that jazz players look at them as being more than just chords. They often have a melodic content. In other words, you can often hear a melody on the top string as you change chords. In the next three examples, listen to the top note in each chord and how it combines with top notes in the other chords to make a melody.

EXAMPLE 32

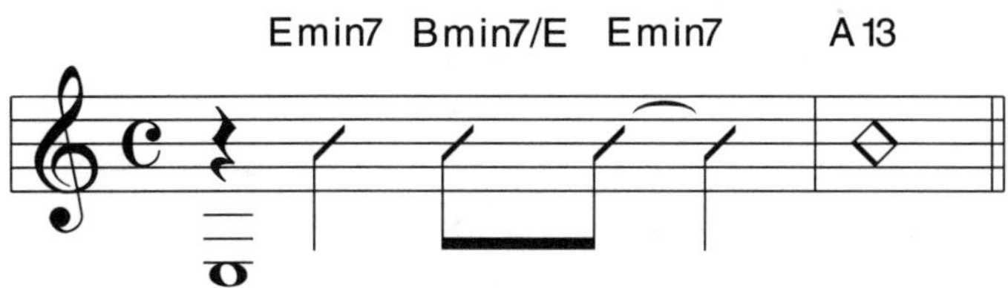

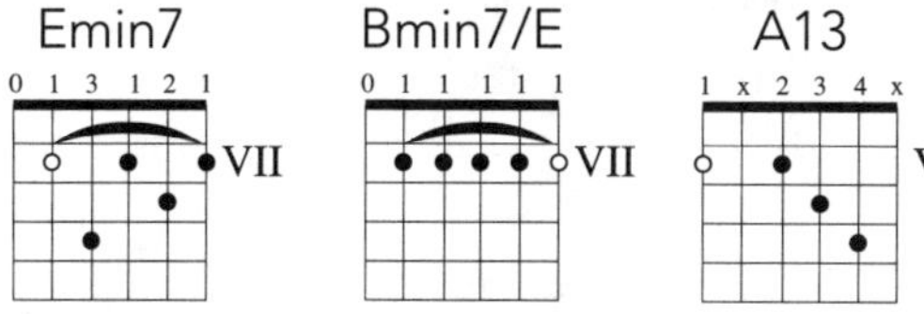

EXAMPLE 33

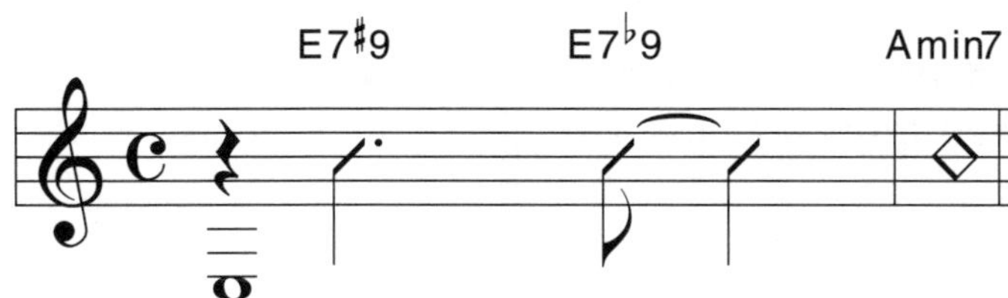

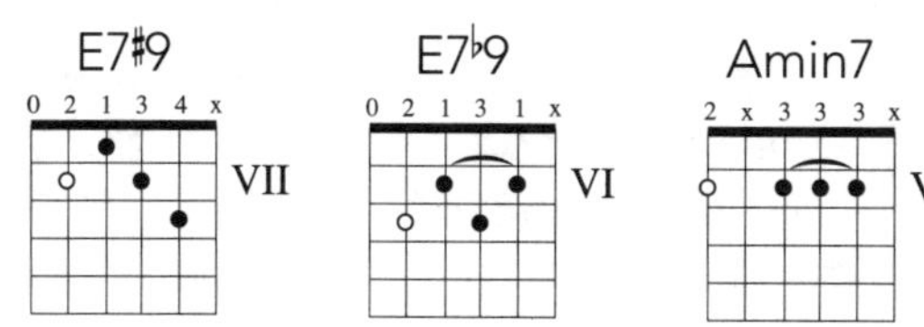

EXAMPLE 34

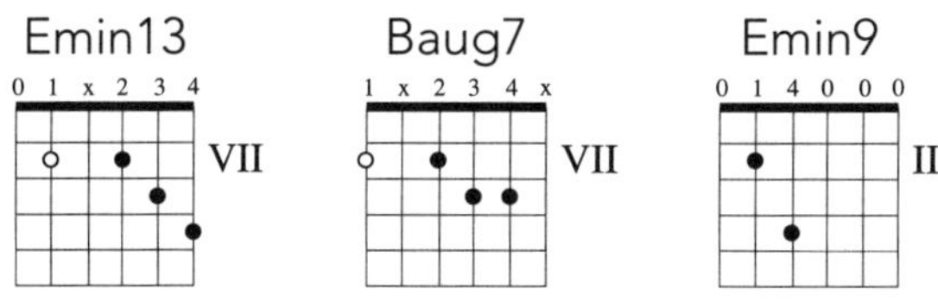

THE ii—V—I PROGRESSION

In jazz, certain kinds of chord progressions seem to occur over and over again. Perhaps the most common of these is the ii—V—I progression. In the key of C, that goes like this:

Dmin7— G7—CMaj7
iimin7— V7— IMaj7

This is a iimin7—V7—IMaj7 in the key of C. These three chords define the key of C, and, in fact, the ii—V—I progression defines the tonality of whatever key you are in. This is because when we hear the iimin7 followed by the V7 there is a very powerful harmonic pull towards the I chord.

Why? First, let's reduce these chords to their components. The two most important notes in each chord are the 3rd and the 7th. These two notes define the quality, or type, of the chord. What they do, and how they move, in a ii—V—I is amazing.

> ***The ♭3 of the iimin7 chord turns into the ♭7 of the V7 chord and then moves down a half-step to become the 3rd of the I chord.***
>
> ***At the same time, the ♭7 of the iimin7 chord moves down a half-step to become the 3rd of the V chord, then turns into the 7 of the IMaj7 chord!***

Really, it is not all that complicated!! Look at the chart:

iimin7	(Dmin7)		**V7**	(G7)		**IMaj7**	(CMaj7)
♭3	(F)	becomes	♭7	(F)	moves to	3	(E)
♭7	(C)	moves to	3	(B)	becomes	7	(B)

Movement between 3rds and 7ths in a ii—V—I progression

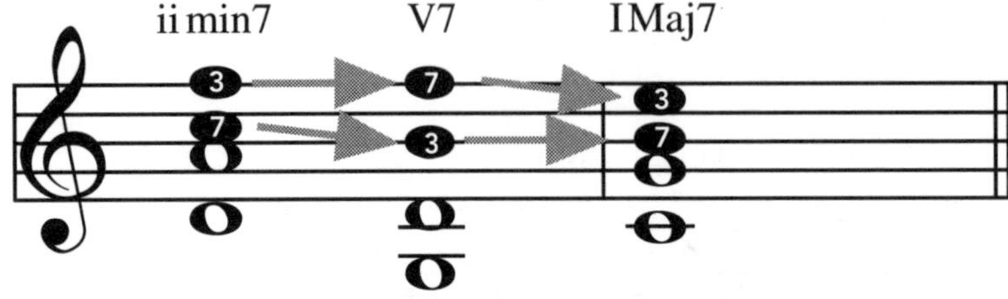

It is this movement between the 3rds and the 7ths that really give us the sound of any key.

EXAMPLES FOR PRACTICING iimin7—V7—IMAJ7

Here are two examples for you to practice to really get the sound of the iimin7—V7—IMaj7 progression in your ears, and the fingerings under your fingers.

Use these voicings for Example 35:

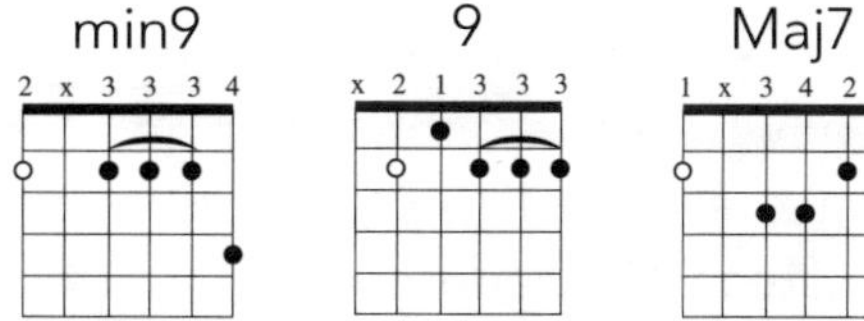

EXAMPLE 35

Start with Fmin9 in thirteenth position.

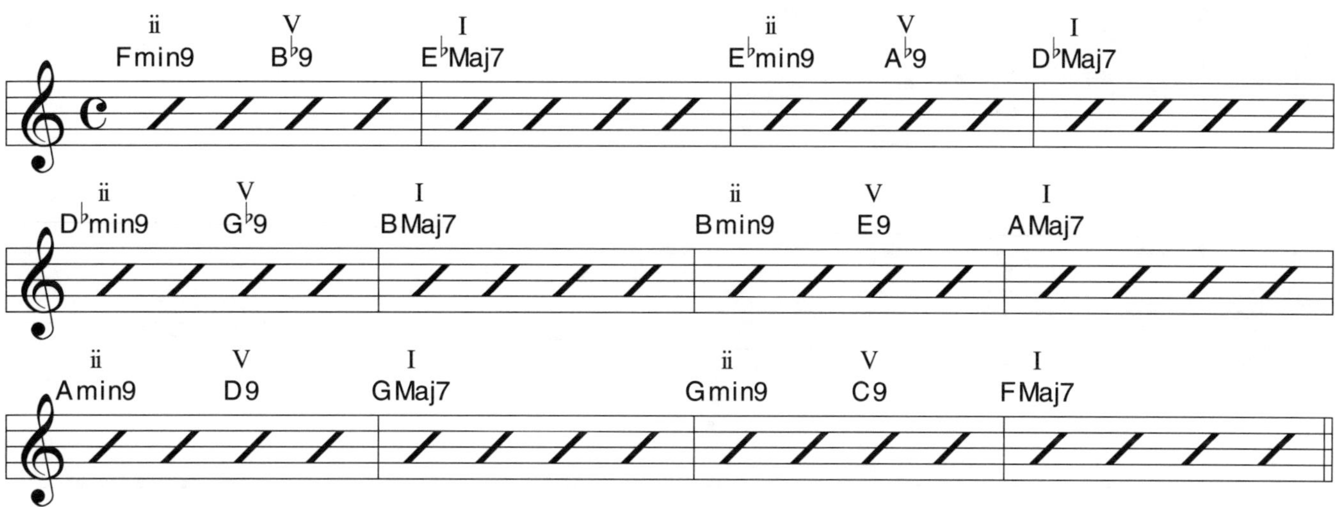

The Exercise 36 is basically the same as Example 35 except the chord voicings are different:

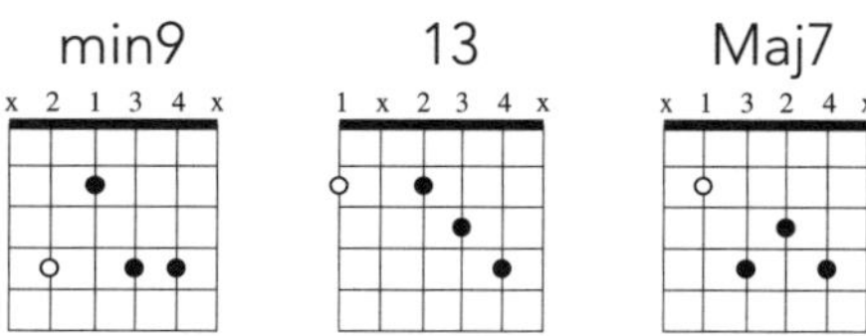

EXAMPLE 36

Start on Cmin9 in thirteenth position.

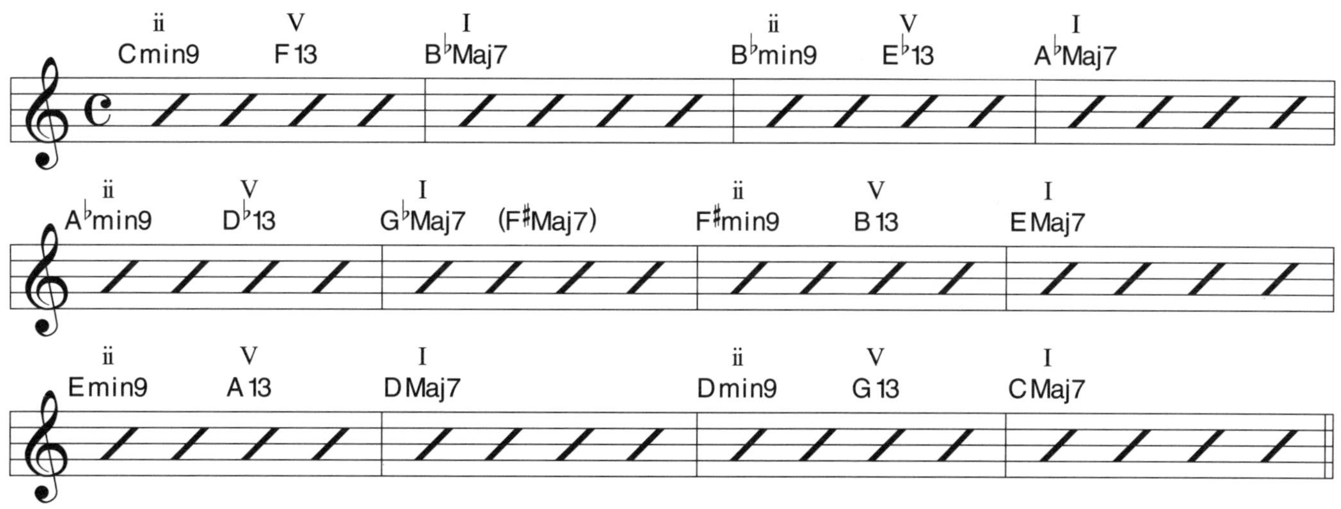

SOLOING OVER iimin7—V7—IMAJ7

Now that you've gotten the sound of the iimin7—V7—IMaj7 in your ears, you need to know what to play over this progression. Here are three possibilities. Examples 37 and 38 start with an ascending Gmin7 arpeggio and then go on to nail the 3rd of the C9 (E) on the first beat of the chord change. That is an excellent idea because you really hear the chord change when you land on that 3rd. Example 39 also lands on the 3rd of the C9, and has an opening Gmin7 arpeggio that is descending instead of ascending.

EXAMPLE 37

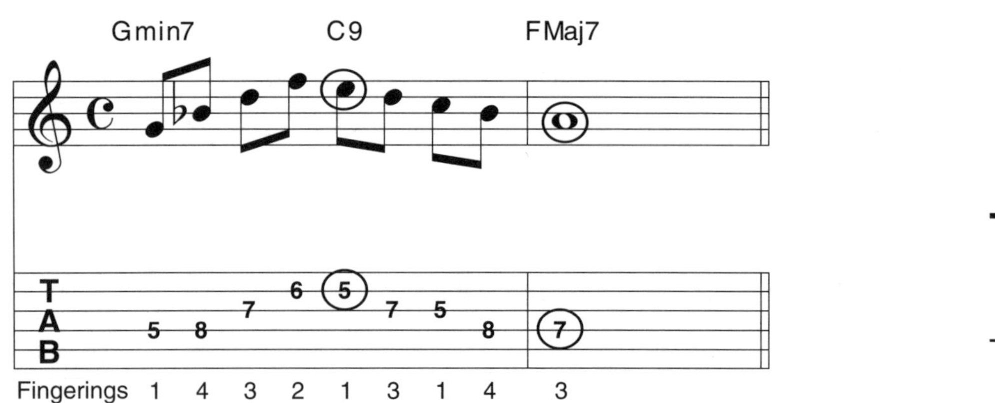

(circled note) = 3rd of the chord
str. = stretch
→ = shift

EXAMPLE 38

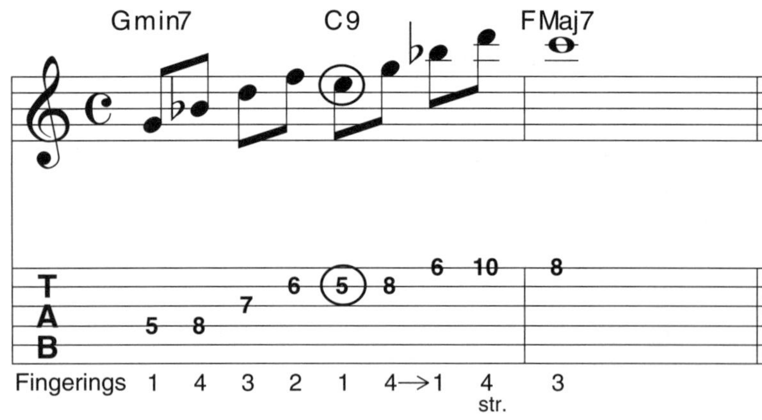

EXAMPLE 39

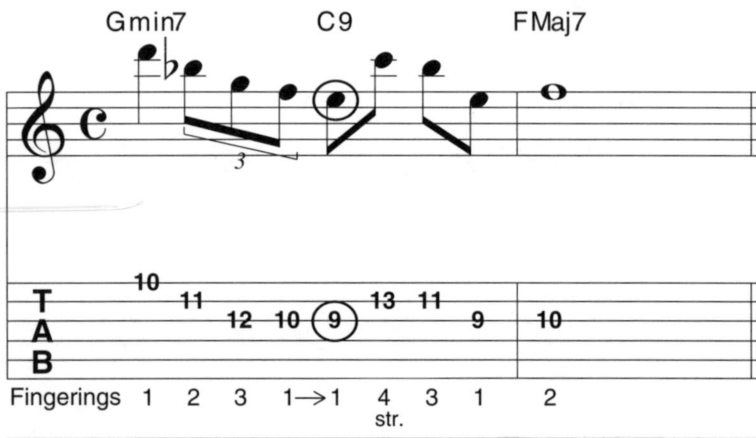

SOLO LICKS FOR iimin7♭5—V7♭9—I

You will often see the ii—V—I expressed as a iimin7♭5—V7♭9—IMaj7 (or imin7 in a minor key) in order to add more tension, or color, to the chords. The interesting thing is that the ♭5 of the ii chord is the same note as the ♭9 of the V chord.

Dmin7♭5		D	F	A♭	C
		1	3	♭5	♭7
G7♭9	G	B	D	F	A♭
	1	3	5	♭7	♭9

Here are three iimin7♭5—V7♭9—IMaj7 (or imin7) lines that you can transpose into any key and play. To transpose, just change your starting note, and play the same fingerings.

EXAMPLE 40

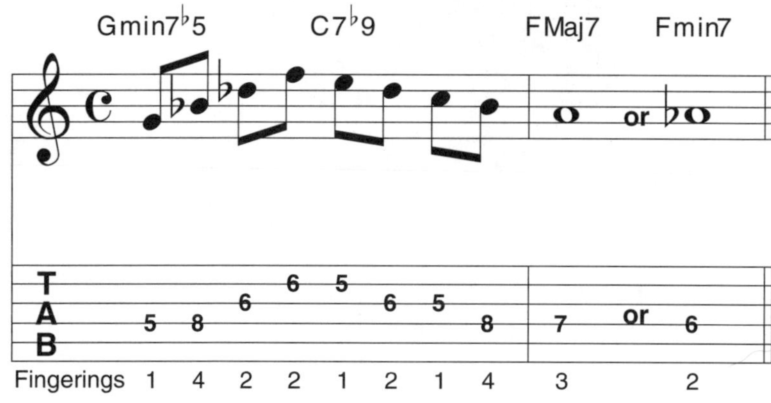

EXAMPLE 41

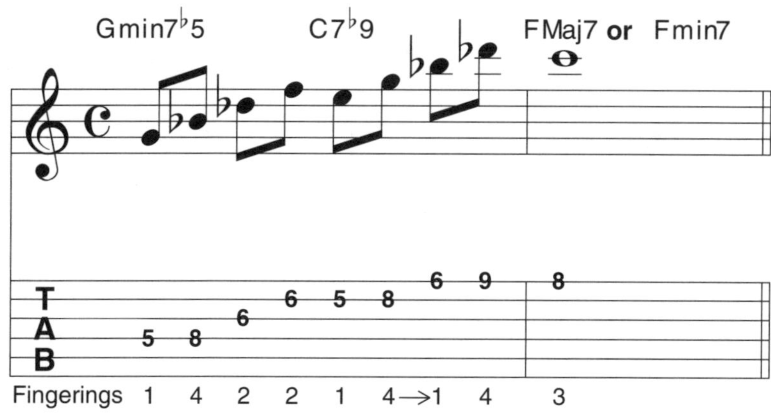

EXAMPLE 42

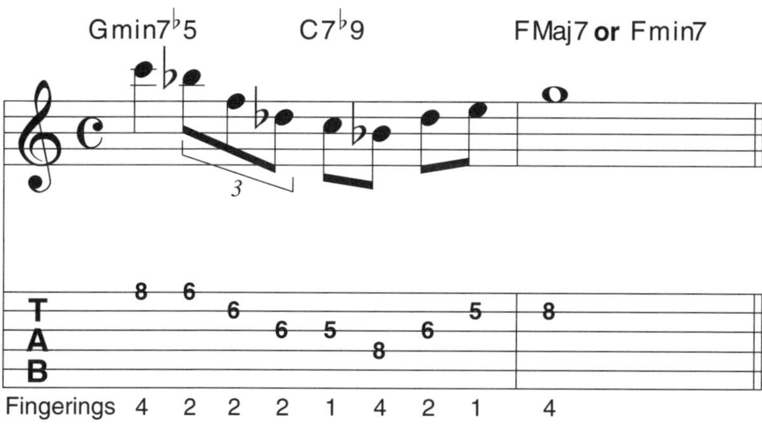

THE TWELVE-BAR BLUES

PHOTO • INSTITUTE OF JAZZ STUDIES

Wes Montgomery

Now here is a chord progression that you probably already know! It is often used in rock and blues songs. Jazz musicians love to use this form, too.

Let's review the form of this progression. It has a very formal structure that follows these rules:

1. It must be twelve measures long. It can be twelve measures of 4/4 time or 12/8, or whatever meter you want!

2. The I, IV, and V chords are all dominant chords. 9ths, 13ths, altered dominant 7ths are included.

3. The first chord of the fifth measure is always a IV7 chord.

4. The last two measures can have a turnaround in them, of which there are many different varieties. The turnaround creates a feeling of coming back around to the I chord.

5. The first chord is always a I7 chord, and the last chord is always a V7 chord.

The standard I—IV—V twelve-bar blues progression EXAMPLE 43

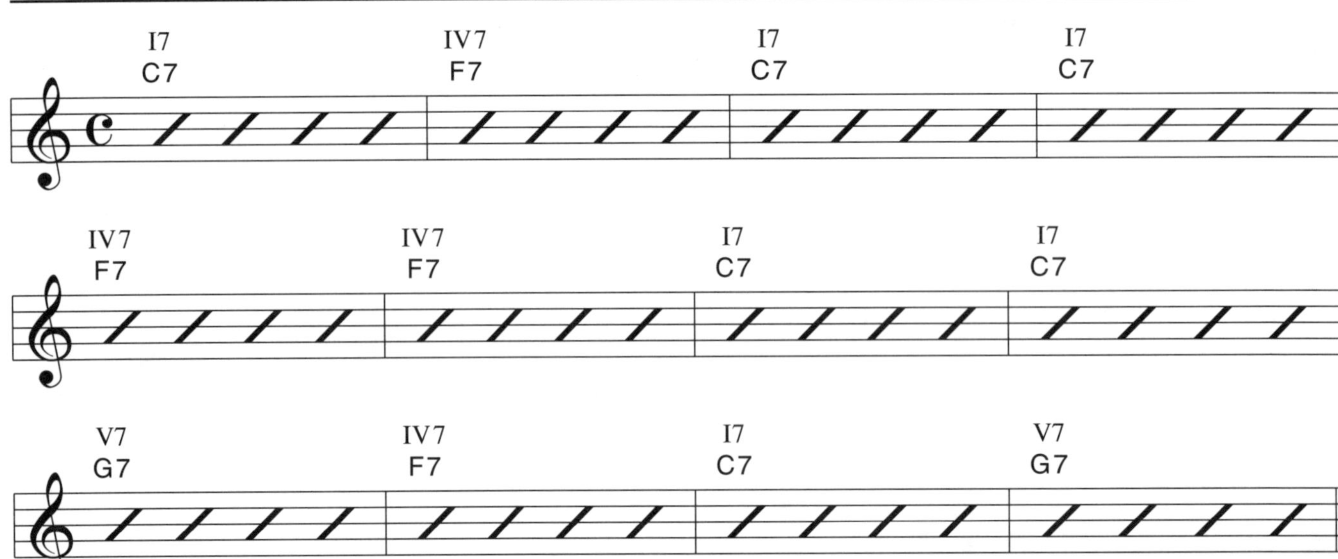

JAZZIER TWELVE-BAR BLUES PROGRESSIONS

You can make that standard **I—IV—V** twelve-bar progression into a hipper sounding blues by using chord substitutions that make the chords more colorful. You can also use passing chords to move smoothly from one chord to the next, such as the Caug7 in measure four of Example 44, and the B♭13 in measure seven. There is also a common turnaround in the last two bars, and the hippest chord change in the whole thing is that F♯dim7 in measure six!

EXAMPLE 44

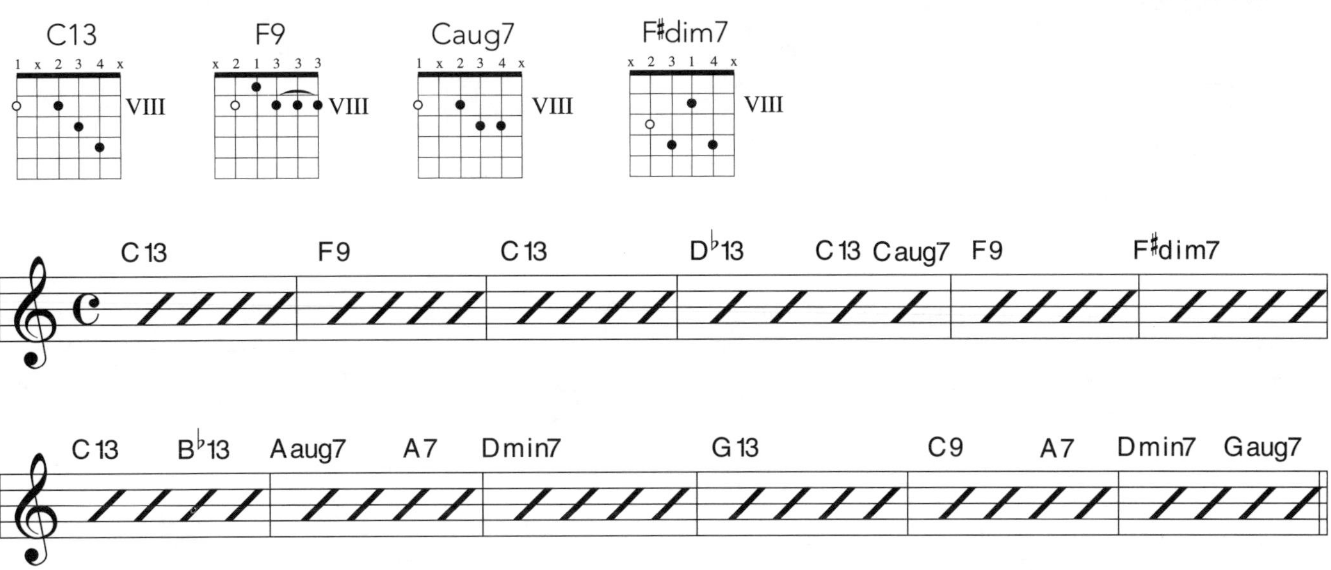

A la the Allman Brothers

EXAMPLE 45

The Allman Brothers did a version of "Stormy Monday" that has some cool chord changes in it. They also used the sliding trick on the 9th chord that we looked at on page 26. Notice how they start to move up the neck in measure seven. Also, notice the use of the Fmin7 in measure ten instead of the usual **V7** chord.

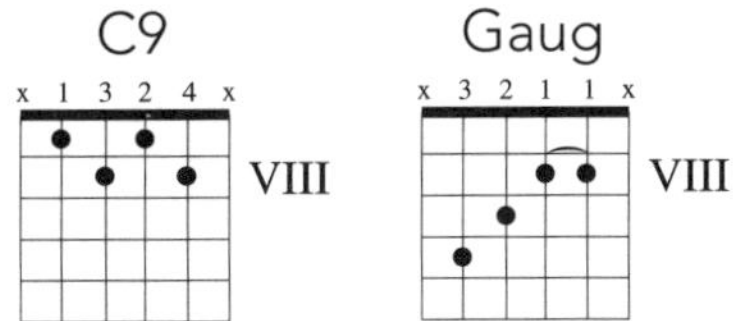

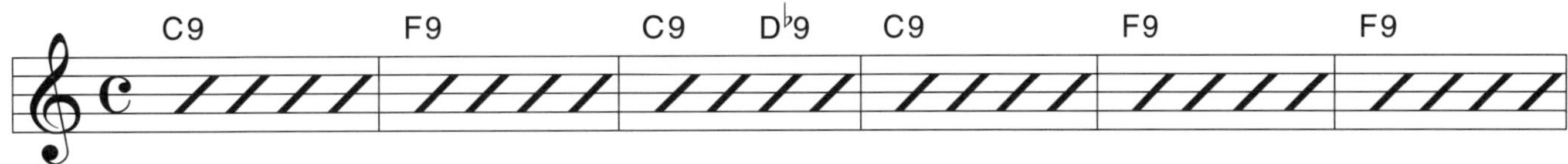

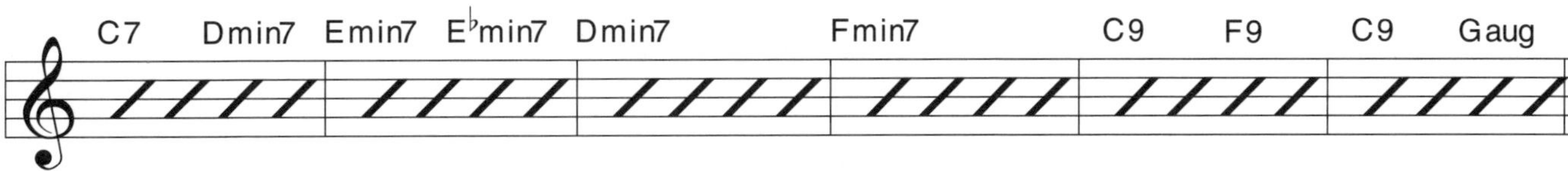

THE SLICKEST TWELVE-BAR BLUES

Here is the slickest, jazziest version of the twelve-bar blues yet! The voicings are really hip, and the walking bass-line in the last four measures makes you sound like two people! By the way, neither the F♯aug7♭9 nor the F♯7♭9 have a root in the voicings shown here. Let the bass player play the root.

Here are the spellings for these very cool chords:

F♯aug7♭9	B♭	E	G	D
	3	♭7	♭9	♯5
F♯7♭9	B♭	E	G	C♯
	3	♭7	♭9	5

Use these voicings:

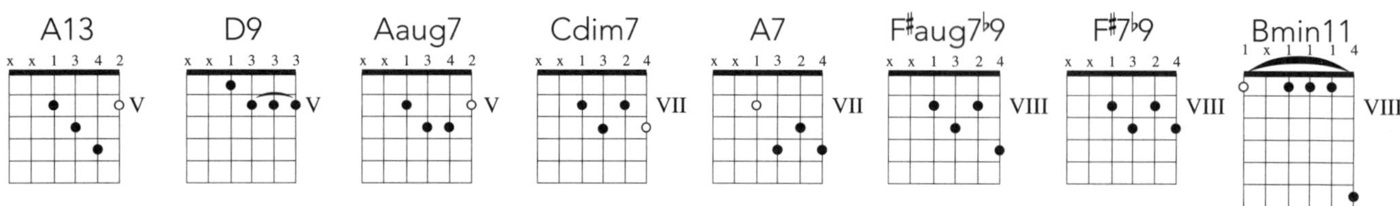

The slickest twelve-bar blues!

EXAMPLE 46

PENTATONICS AND THE BLUES

We usually use the minor pentatonic scale to solo over blues changes. Here's the most commonly used fingering:

A Minor Pentatonic scale

EXAMPLE 47

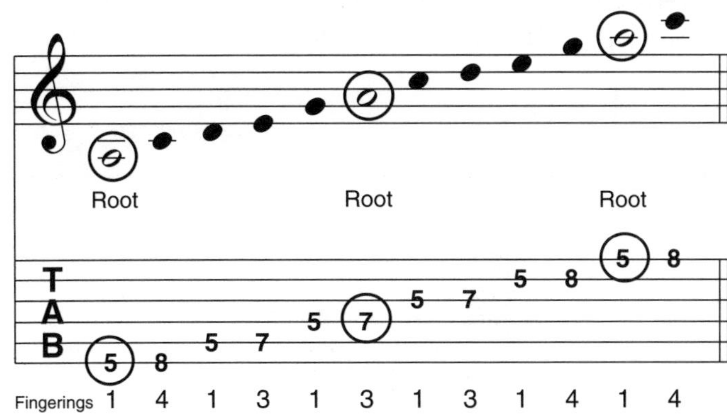

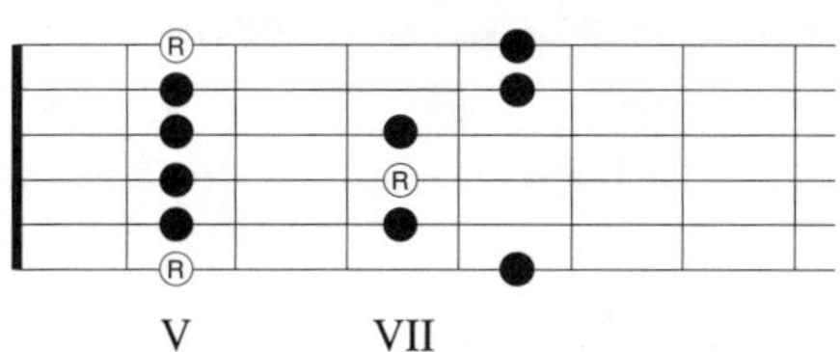

If you move down three frets and play the same minor pentatonic fingering, you will be playing the major pentatonic scale for the same key!!

A Major Pentatonic scale

EXAMPLE 48

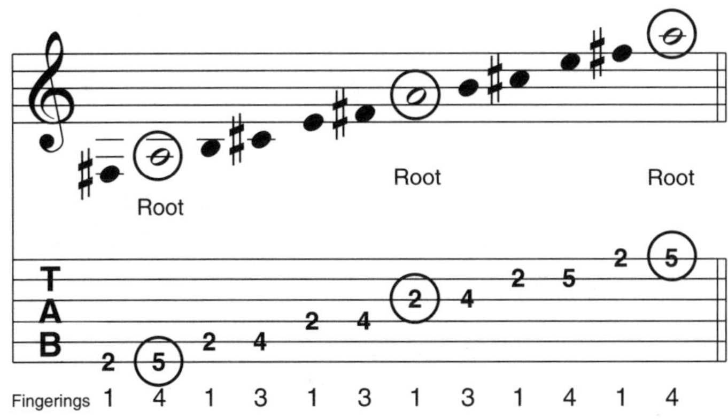

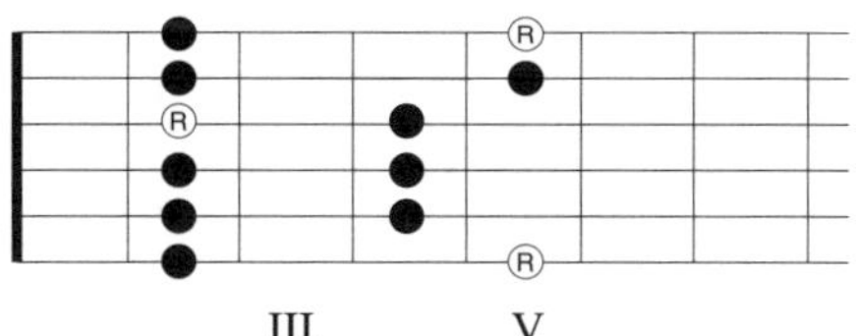

You can even jazz up the major pentatonic scale by adding a few passing tones, which are notes that are not found in the chord or, sometimes, even in the key.

A Major Pentatonic with passing tones

EXAMPLE 49

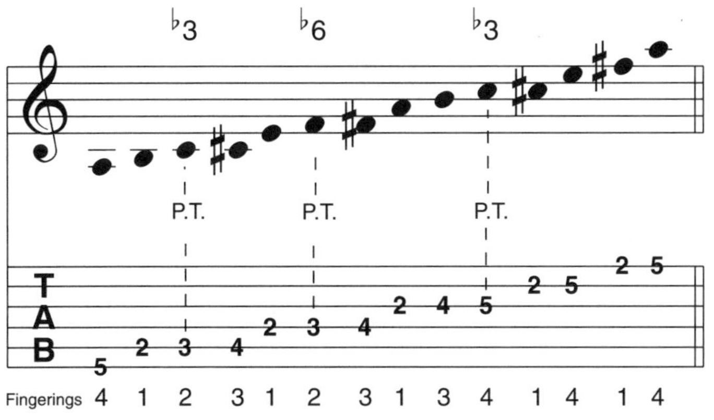

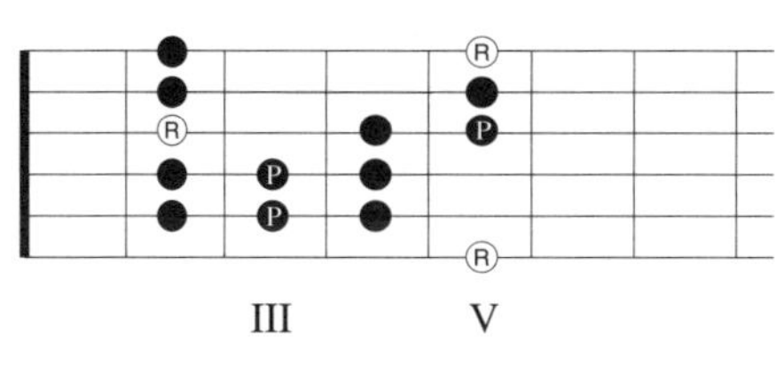

P.T. = } Passing tone
P =

PENTATONIC DERIVATIVES

After playing your the pentatonic scale for a while, you will probably get bored with it, right? That's probably one of the reasons you are reading this book! You can jazz it up with the following three scales. They are all based on the minor pentatonic scale. The first one adds a ♭5 and takes away the ♭7. The second minor pentatonic derivative puts the ♭7 back in, and keeps the ♭5. The third scale is called a hybrid scale because the first half of it is different from the second half.

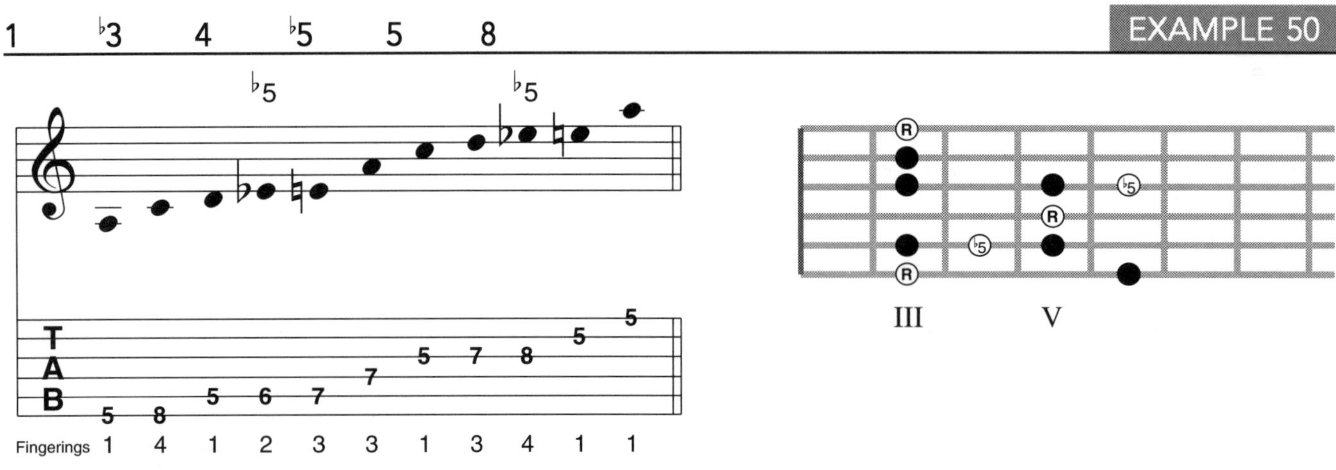

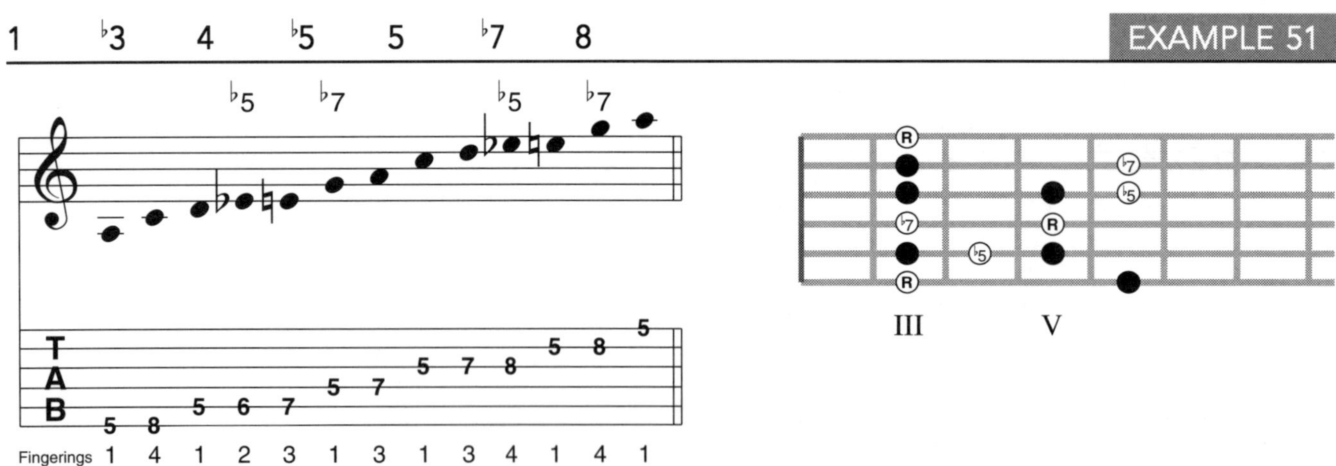

Here is a hybrid pentatonic scale.

First half 1 ♭3 4 ♭5 5 ♭7 ♮7
Second half 1 ♭3 4 ♭5 5 6 ♭7 1 9 ♭3

EXAMPLE 52

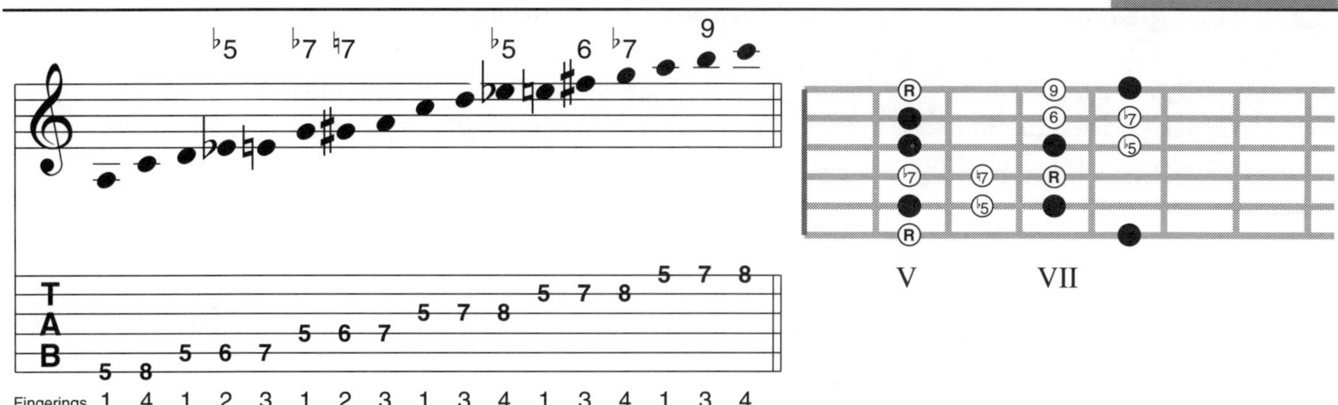

PHOTO: NATHANIEL WELCH/COURTESY BLUEMOON

Scott Henderson

TARGET NOTES AND CHORD TONES

"Hitting the *target notes*" is a very important concept for single-note soloing over chord changes. Landing on important notes from the chords will give you a jazzier sound and make you sound like a pro.

We know that the most important notes in any chord are the 3rd and the 7th. The root and the color notes, such as 9ths and 13ths, would be next in importance. Let's say you are playing a twelve-bar blues in A, and you are playing minor pentatonic licks based on all those cool scales you have just learned. There is a D9 in the second bar. Try to land on one of the important notes—one of the target notes—on the first beat of the second measure. A great note to hit there is the F♯, which is the 3rd of the D9 chord.

EXAMPLE 53

In this example the notes walk down in triplets from the A7 chord right into the F♯ target note for the D9 on the first beat of measure two!

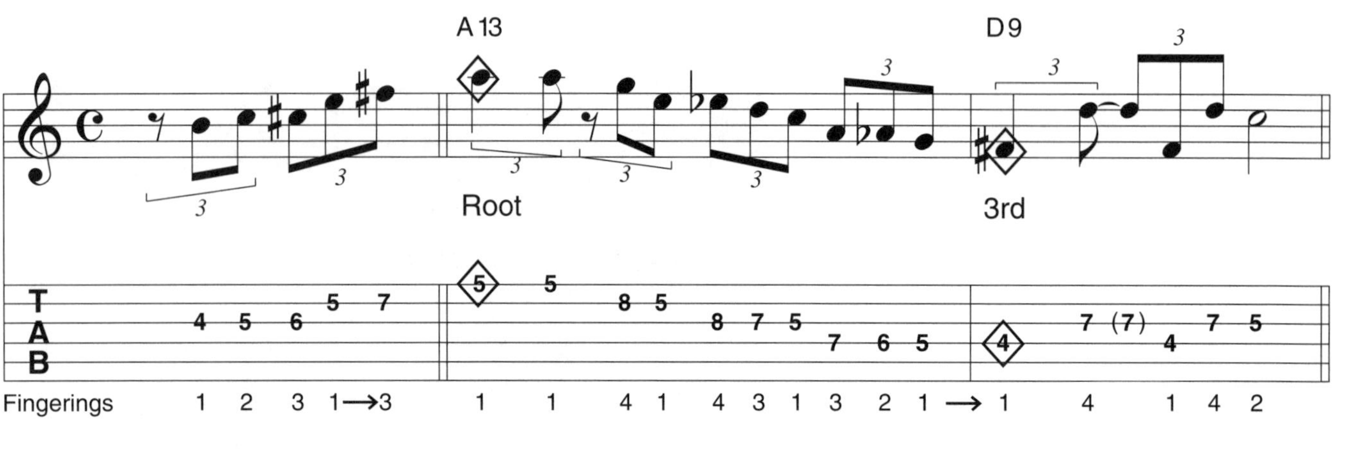

◇ = Target note

Another important idea for jazz improvising is to use the notes right out of the chord shape you are playing—the *chord tones*. For instance, the voicing given below for a D13 chord could be the basis for a line such as the one in Example 54.

EXAMPLE 54

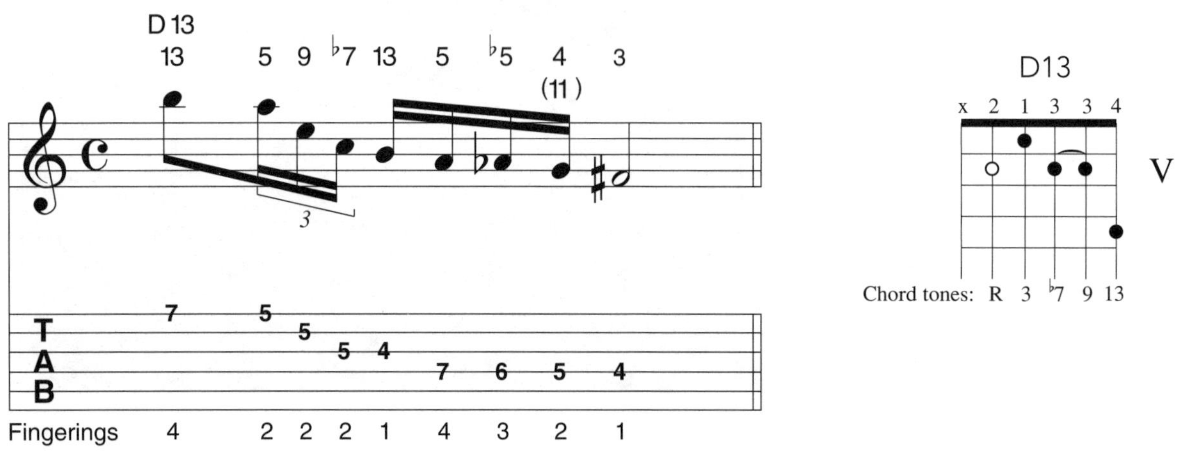

Here are three examples showing different approaches to target notes. It's a good idea to start on a "color note," such as a 9th or a 13th. Look at the first beat of the second measure in all three examples—each one is a chord tone.

EXAMPLE 55

This example works over a iimin7—V7 progression and starts on the 9th of the ii chord (Dmin9).

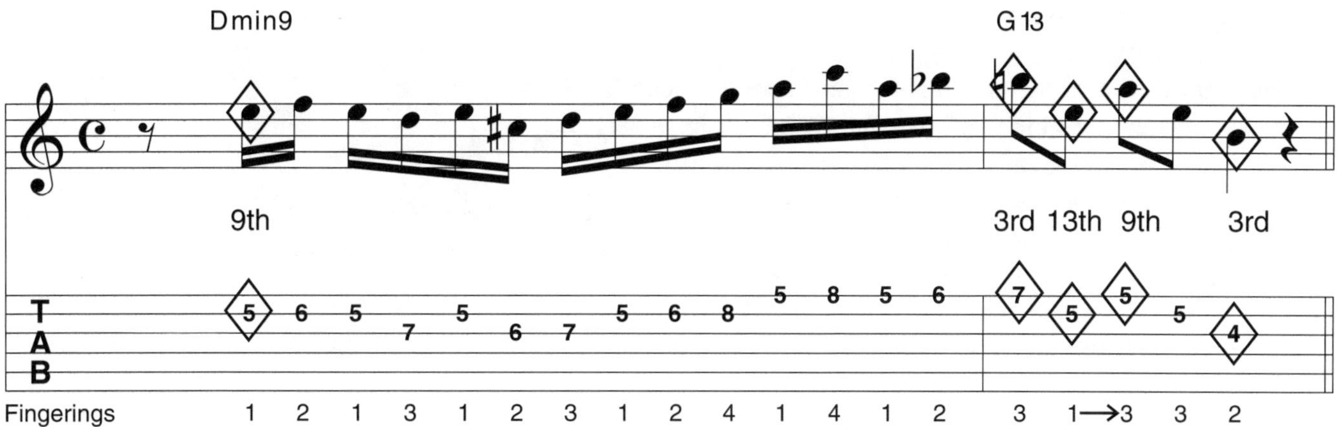

EXAMPLE 56

This example uses a triplet figure to walk down from E13 into A7. Each triplet traces a triad.

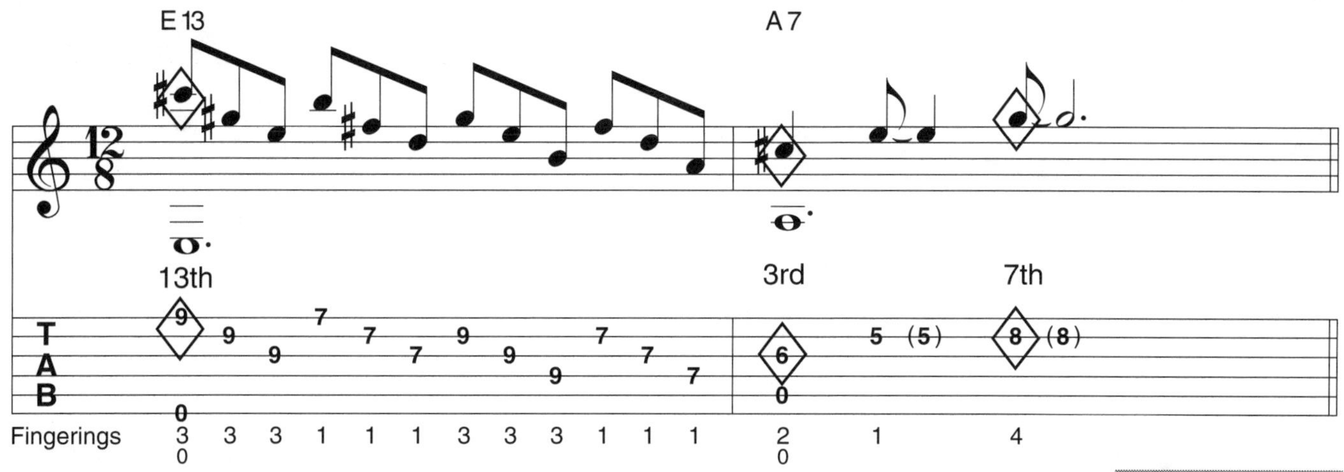

EXAMPLE 57

This is a great example of outlining chords in a solo line!

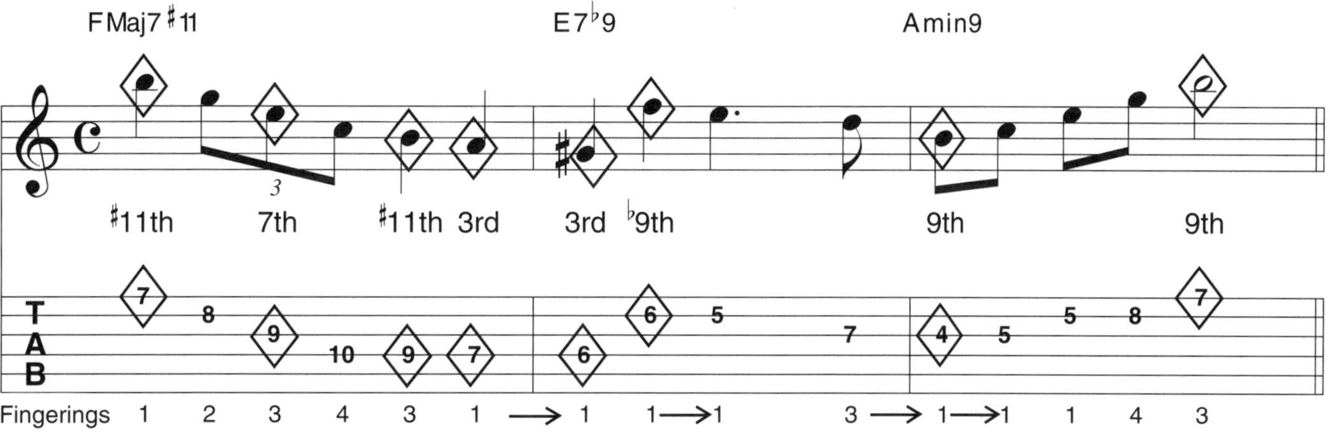

JAZZ IN A MINOR KEY

We have covered two kinds of minor scales in this book: natural minor and the Dorian mode. There are many others for you to explore. For now, let's learn how to determine which of these two you should use to improvise when playing over a minor chord progression. Look at this progression: **Gmin7—Amin7—Dmin7.**

We could try D Minor Pentatonic first, and that would work. But that seems kind of limiting. Which minor scale could we play over this? One way to figure this out is to analyze the chords to see how they fit into the diatonic 7th chords for major keys (see page 18). These three chords, as it turns out, are in the key of F Major, because that is the only key that has min7 chords with the roots G, A and D.

In F Major:		
Gmin7	Amin7	Dmin7
iimin7	**iiimin7**	**vimin7**

We should be able to play a G Dorian mode over these chords, because the G Dorian mode is the same as the F Major scale played starting on G. And, all the diatonic chords from the F Major scale are G Dorian chords, too!

F Major scale	F	G	A	B♭	C	D	E	F	
G Dorian mode		G	A	B♭	C	D	E	F	G

EXAMPLE 58

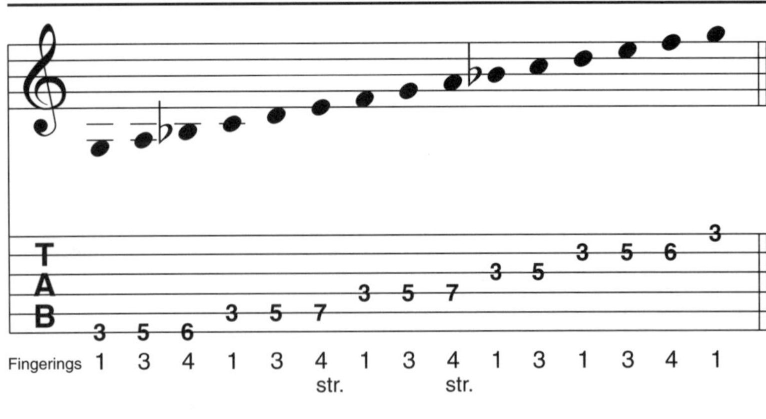

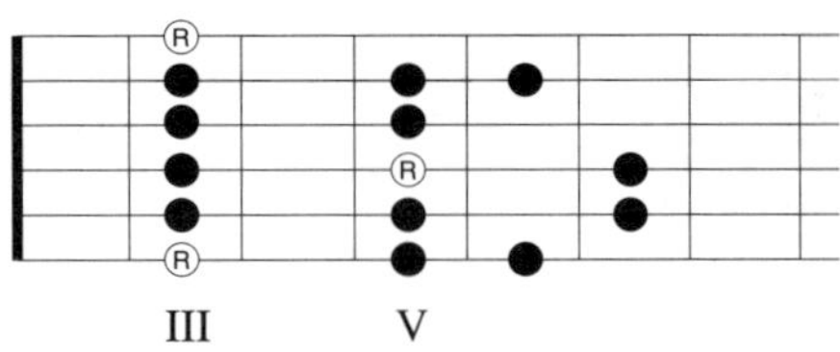

EXAMPLE 59

Using the same logic, we can play a D Natural Minor scale (see page 11) over these same chords.

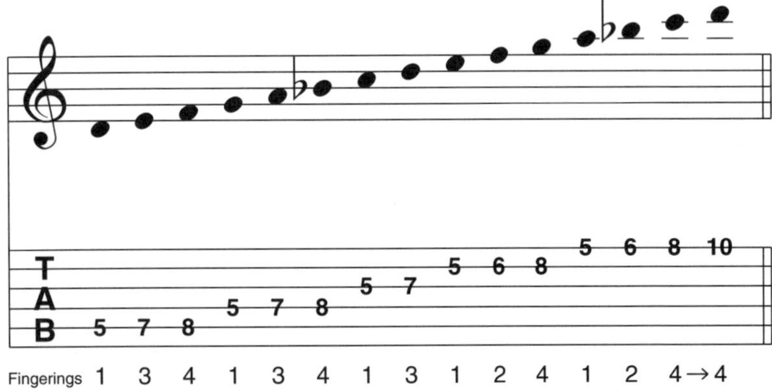

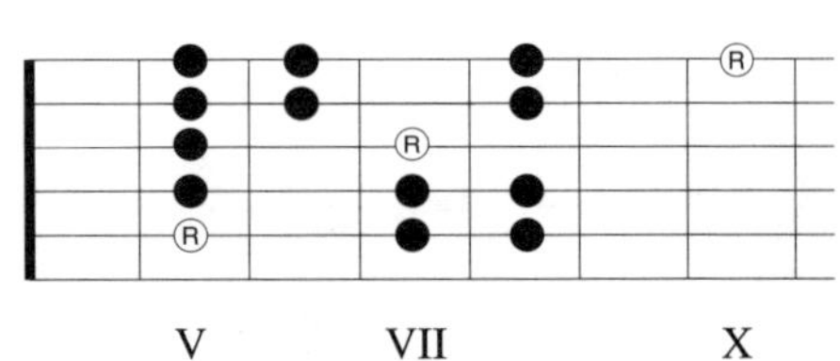

Continuing with the Gmin7—Amin7—Dmin7 chord progression, here are three excellent lines that really show off the character of the Dorian mode. These hot licks go perfectly with each chord. Notice the target notes which fall on the strong beats of each measure, where the chords change. You also might try playing these lines in some other keys—the fingerings will be the same!

EXAMPLE 60

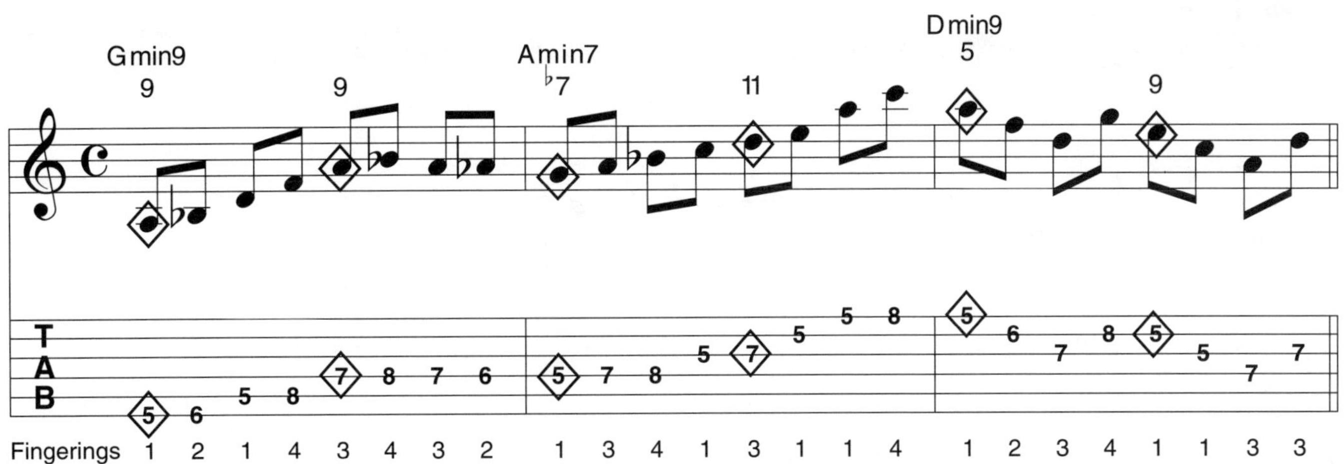

EXAMPLE 61

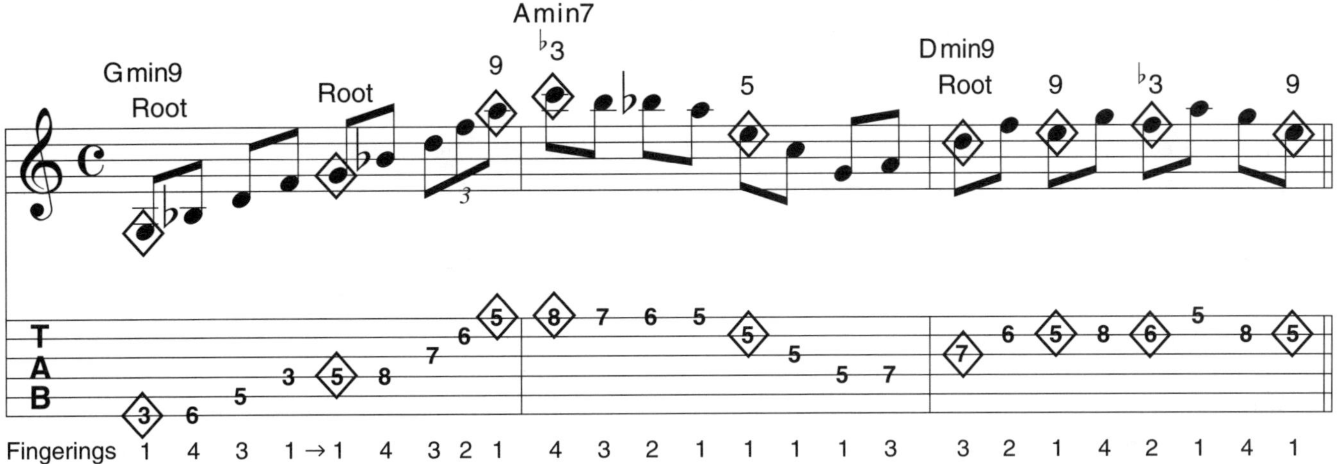

EXAMPLE 62

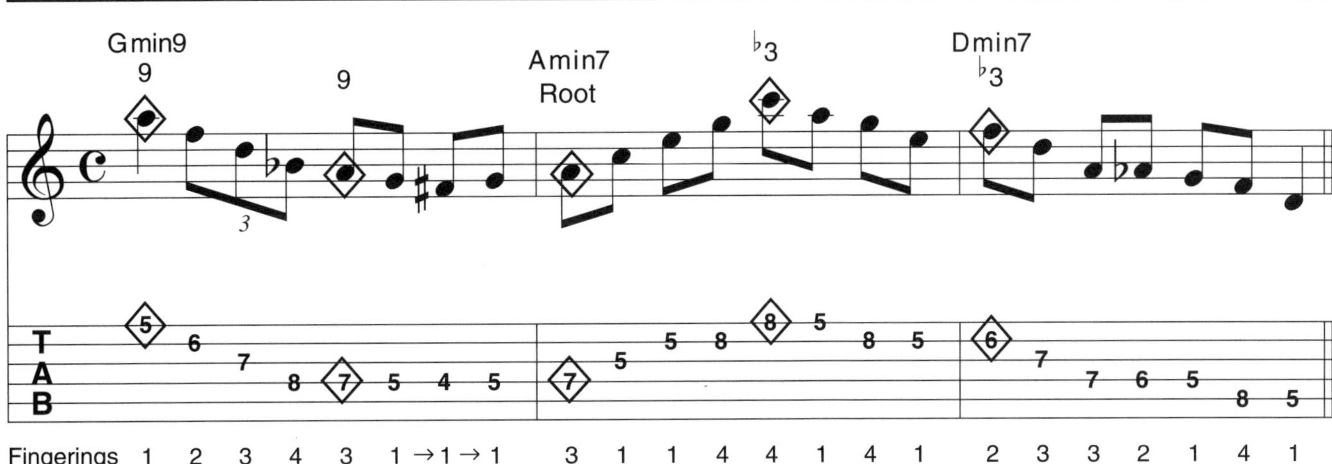

WHERE DO YOU GO FROM HERE?

Here are some suggestions that I hope will help as you continue studying jazz guitar.

1. Find a jazz guitar teacher. If there isn't one in your area, any other jazz musician—a piano player, sax player, etc.—can help you understand jazz concepts.

2. Find a bass player to jam with at least once a week. Play jazz standards together. You'll soon find out that the role of the guitar player in this situation is one of responsibility—you have to do most of the work!

3. Listen to lots of jazz recordings. Don't restrict yourself to guitar players either. Most of them learned how to play by listening to sax and trumpet players!

4. Have patience. There is no secret formula other than practice, practice, and more practice.

5. Take some classes about jazz improvising, technique and theory such as those offered at the National Guitar Workshop. There's a ton of information out there for those who seek it out.

7. There are many other instructional books on the market. They can be of significant value to you if you buy wisely and know what you want to get out of each book. I urge you to check out the *Stand Alone* practice cassettes and CDs published by the National Guitar Workshop and Alfred, especially *Stand Alone Jazz*. They are great practice tools. Remember, though, there is no real substitute for a teacher.

8. Transcribe and learn to play solos and melodies that you hear on recordings. Start with easier ones and be patient. It often takes hours to get sixteen bars of solo learned and written out. Writing it down is a very important step that should not be left out.

9. See as much live jazz as you can. A lot of it is free. And listen to the radio. There is almost always jazz somewhere on the air-waves.

10. Start to develop your own approach to music. Finding your own way of playing any tune in any style is important. It is *not* important how well you can play this person or that person's version of a tune. You study it to learn something about how to approach the music. Go for the concepts, not the exact notes. Your style may be a mix of everything you have ever played. There are many great guitarists who blend rock, country, jazz, and R&B into one cohesive, seamless way to play music. Check it out and have fun!

READING MUSIC AND TABLATURE

STANDARD MUSIC NOTATION

Reading standard music notation is a necessary skill for anyone interested in learning to play jazz. Once you get the idea, you'll find that it's really easy, and then a whole world of instructional books and great music will open up for you. There are two basic elements to standard notation: *pitch* and *rhythm*. Every note has a particular note name (pitch) and particular duration (rhythm). The specific line or space on which the note falls tells you the pitch.

Every song has numbers at the beginning, called the time signature, that tell us how to count the time. The top number represents the number of beats or counts per *measure*. The bottom number represents the type of note receiving one count. The most common time signature, 4/4, is shown below. In 4/4 time, there are four beats per measure, and the quarter note (♩) receives one beat.

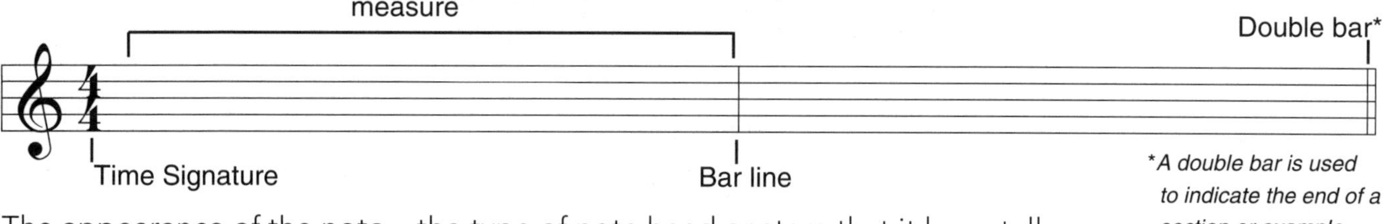

**A double bar is used to indicate the end of a section or example.*

The appearance of the note—the type of note head or stem that it has—tells you the rhythm. Finally, rests tell you when and for how long not to play, which is also an important aspect of rhythm. Here are the note vales in 4/4 time:

Whole rest 4 beats
Half rest 2 beats
Quarter rest 1 beat
Eighth rest 1/2 beat
Sixteenth rest 1/4 beat

Whole note 4 beats
Half note 2 beats
Quarter note 1 beat
Eighth note 1/2 beat
Sixteenth note 1/4 beat

TABLATURE

Tablature is a system of notation that graphically represents the strings and frets of the guitar fingerboard. Each note is indicated by placing a number, which indicates the fret to play, on the appropriate string.

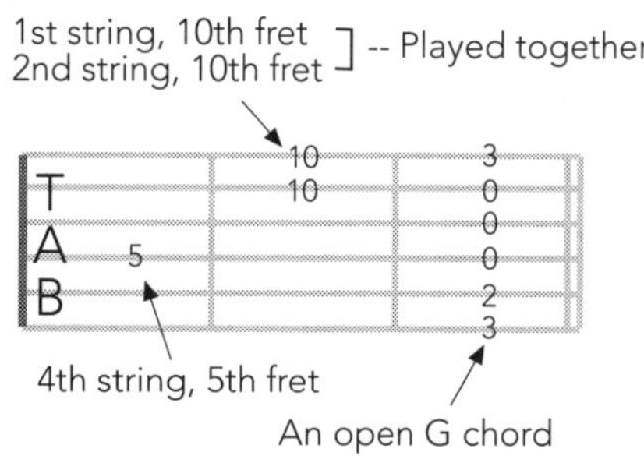